JB JOSSEY-BASS™
A Wiley Brand

T0314932

Fundraising for Beginners

Essential Procedures for Getting a Fundraising Program Up and Running

Scott C. Stevenson, Editor

WILEY

Fundraising for Beginners

Essential Procedures for Getting a Fundraising Program
Up and Running

Published by

Stevenson, Inc.

P.O. Box 4528 • Sioux City, Iowa • 51104
Phone 712.239.3010 • Fax 712.239.2166
www.stevensoninc.com

TABLE OF CONTENTS

TABLE OF CONTENTS

Fundraising for Beginners: Essential Procedures for Getting a Fundraising Program Up and Running.
Edited by Scott C. Stevenson.
© 2009 Stevenson, Inc. Published 2009 by Stevenson, Inc.

YOUR FRAME OF MIND IS KEY TO SUCCESS

When it comes to raising funds, frame of mind matters. The first step in achieving fundraising success requires exhibiting a passion for your cause. A can-do attitude and your ability to overcome call reluctance will make a significant difference. It's equally important to know your product inside and out.

How You View Fundraising Makes a Difference

How many times have your heard someone say, "How can you beg people for money?" Not exactly reassuring, is it?

If you're new to the development profession and troubled by asking for gifts, you may be viewing your role as a professional fundraiser in the wrong light. If you honestly believe in the cause for which you are working (and that's an important "if"), then you're not a beggar, you're a broker.

You are a broker of dreams — helping your nonprofit realize its dreams, helping prospects fulfill their dreams. You, the professional fundraiser, are the means to the end.

In a sense, you're a matchmaker.

What greater reward is there in life than helping others? You are providing individuals with the opportunity to help. You are helping donors to help society in their own special ways.

So don't make excuses or feel apologetic about soliciting gifts for your cause, for your role provides you with the rare opportunity of making dreams come true. Once you truly believe that, your ability to sell your cause will be elevated dramatically, and so, too, will gifts to your organization.

It's Important to Nurture a Positive Attitude

Most sales performance problems are caused by lack of the right attitude rather than lack of sales skills. Potential is not truly effective unless it is driven by a winning attitude.

Here are steps to take to strengthen and maintain a positive attitude:

1. Take note of the total number of solicitation calls you make during the course of a week or month, not just the number of gifts or pledges you receive. It's been proven time and again that, on average, it takes a certain number of rejections before making a successful sale. Whatever that average is for you, accept it and take comfort in the fact that you're making contacts frequently and regularly. When you get discouraged, keep in mind: The more contacts you make, the better the odds of securing a gift!

2. Maintain a "steady as she goes" point of view. Just as you should not get too caught up in a successful solicitation call, don't dwell on an unsuccessful attempt to secure a new gift. There are many external factors that impact giving, some of which we have no control over. Don't dwell on misfortune; move ahead.

3. Be enthusiastic about solicitation strategies brought to the table, old and new. Whether it's a new direct mail idea or an old solicitation strategy that was rejected a year ago, it may be just the approach your organization needs right now. Plus, when you greet all ideas enthusiastically, you encourage others to bring more ideas to you.

4. Look for good qualities in people, not negative ones. If you focus on positive aspects of colleagues, volunteers and prospects, your attitude will serve as a mirror in bringing out the best in others — whether it's greater productivity, a willingness to do more for your agency, or saying "yes" to your gift request. By stressing people's good points, you'll be taken more seriously by those with whom you come in contact. People tend to react positively to positive direction.

Convince Yourself: It Will Happen

If you believe it's unlikely your charity could one day receive a seven- or even eight-figure gift, you're probably right. It will never happen.

If, however, you convince yourself that a mega gift will be made — it's just a matter of when and by whom — the odds of that happening are greatly increased.

Whether it's securing a major gift, doubling the number of donors or recruiting the board member who is the envy of every nonprofit around, believe that it can and will happen. Then develop and implement a plan to make it so.

Overcome Call Reluctance

Excuse: "If I ask, I might hear 'no.'"

Advice: Ask and you may receive. Don't ask and you won't. You'll never hear "yes" if you don't ask.

Excuse: "I hate asking for money."

Advice: Most people like and expect to be asked to support worthy causes.

YOUR FRAME OF MIND IS KEY TO SUCCESS

Do What's Right and Positive Results Will Follow

Part of feeling positive about yourself and your work is doing the right things and devoting sufficient time to them — even if you may not be doing them perfectly.

Use the development responsibilities analysis form below to assess how you've been spending your time. Measure the results against your job description and objectives established for/by you and your department. Recognizing where you're on target and where you may fall short will illustrate behavioral changes that need to take place.

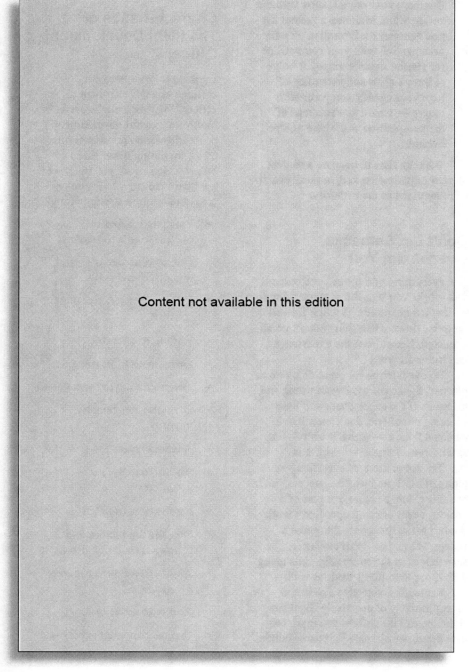

Content not available in this edition

Attitude Matters

Tell yourself that you have 100 gifts waiting to happen over the next 30 days. But they won't happen without you taking action.

Some gifts will require personal visits. Others, phone calls. Still others, personal handwritten correspondence or e-mail. Some gifts will require a combination of these actions.

Recognize that the power to bring these gifts to fruition lies within you.

Be Willing to Fail And Learn From The Experience

One of the most important factors separating successful fundraising professionals from others is their willingness to accept failure and move forward.

Many professionals procrastinate when it comes to soliciting gifts. Why? Because they fear rejection. They want to avoid failure. "If I don't ask anyone for a gift, I can't fail."

Ironically, the best advice one could give a reluctant fundraiser is, "Go ahead and fail! It's all right. Feel free to fail over and over again."

As you accept your willingness to fail in soliciting gifts, you begin to learn from your mistakes and strengthen your ability to pursue more gifts. Sales is, in part, a numbers game. The more calls you can make, the more you increase the odds of successfully securing gifts for your organization.

Be willing to accept your inability to successfully close all solicitations. Accept your failures, learn from them, and move on to your next success.

YOUR FRAME OF MIND IS KEY TO SUCCESS

Get to Know Your Product

A sound understanding of your organization's product is indispensable as you sell to prospects who might be willing to invest. Sales skills have little meaning without the ability to understand and explain your product to others.

Additionally, the more you can understand and distinguish your organization's product(s) from other similar organizations, the more sold you become. And when you're sold on the merits of your nonprofit, you'll be much more effective in selling to others!

Make it a practice to regularly broaden your knowledge of your agency and its products. Here are some steps you can take:

❑ Pretend you're the prospect being introduced to an organization for the first time. What questions might you have? What questions would you want answered if you were being asked to make a contribution?

❑ Begin a facts file that you can add to from time to time. Whenever you discover a new piece of information on your organization that you didn't know, jot it down and include it in your facts file.

❑ Make time to regularly visit with your nonprofit's employees on an individual basis. Learn as much as you can about their jobs. Their daily achievements may provide you with valuable sales information.

❑ Compare your organization with the competition. Maintain a factual list that compares information on your organization with your competition (or similar organizations). It helps to have a clear understanding of how your agency compares with others — where you're ahead of the competition and where you're behind.

Take the time to become a student of your organization and, in time, you'll be recognized as the authority.

Don't Let Setbacks Overwhelm You

Not everything you try in development will work. You will fail at some things — that's a guarantee. But don't dwell on those times when things don't go as expected. Learn from the experience and move forward.

If your fundraising event didn't go as planned, figure out what went wrong and try again. If the major donor you were counting on said no, don't view it as a personal failure — which it isn't — but as a business refusal — which it is.

Try not to think of everything in terms of black and white... success or failure. Just because one part of a project, event or campaign didn't work doesn't mean the whole thing was a failure. When you do an evaluation, be sure to look at the successful parts along with those that didn't work as well.

Remember, you have a choice to think positively or negatively about any situation, and the choices you make can help determine ultimate success or failure.

Overcome Your Fear of Failure

Most development professionals experience at least some fear when making calls. The fear of failure — or call reluctance, as it is often referred to — keeps even the most experienced professionals from tackling what they might perceive as a difficult call.

Next time you're faced with this feeling, remember:

• Babe Ruth, over the course of his amazing baseball career, struck out more times than he hit home runs.

• Thomas Edison had 6,000 failures before he invented the electric light bulb.

So even if you do fail once in awhile, remember, you're in very good company.

Learn From Obstacles Along the Way

Just about any project in development will be filled with obstacles to overcome — each presenting an opportunity for growth and learning, if you're willing to look for it.

Characteristics of The Ideal Development Officer

Looking to improve your abilities as a development officer? While no one is perfect, highly successful development professionals do possess similar traits, including those listed below. Gauge how you measure up, then take steps to improve areas that require strengthening.

• Passionate belief in organization's mission.

• Outstanding planning and organizational skills.

• Effective writer, articulate speaker.

• Willing to take risks.

• Genuine and sincere.

• Determination to meet goals.

• Demonstrates honesty, integrity.

• A team player.

• Ability to motivate volunteers.

• Knows how to listen.

• Sees the big picture and follows through on details.

• Ability to relate to different personalities.

• Ability to multi-task.

• Capital campaign experience.

DEVELOP A PLAN OF ACTION

Planning is crucial to fundraising success. A well thought out operational plan, complete with goals, quantifiable objectives, action plans and a year-long calendar will help to ensure your fundraising goals are achieved. This chapter provides a framework for creating a plan and offers some procedures to help you achieve and surpass fundraising goals.

How to Create Your Fundraising Plan

When planning fundraising strategies for your new fiscal year, one of the first steps is to analyze the strengths and weaknesses of the previous year.

"Successful planning requires a focus on the overall goal and the ability to examine strategies objectively, without taking it personally when pet projects or ideas don't make the plan," says Michele Van Dyke, executive director, Luverne Area Community Foundation (Luverne, MN). "Remember strategies wear out just like clothes and need to be replaced with something new regularly."

To build your strategic fundraising plan, Van Dyke suggests inviting staff and board members to an all-day retreat away from your worksite. Options to consider include hiring an independent facilitator or board member with similar skills to help the group stick to the goal and time constraints of the day. Prior to the event, write a focused agenda with timeframes and distribute to all who will attend. Provide everyone with long-range strategy information and plans from previous years.

Van Dyke advises to begin by reviewing your strategic plan from the previous year and discussing the actual outcomes. She feels that is a great way to identify potential for growth and improvement. Stick to timeframes and bring all suggestions back to the office where the strategic plan can be assembled, complete with work plans. If applicable, let each department develop its work plan around its goals and objectives.

As the year progresses, review progress towards goals and objectives monthly and update board members quarterly. Informed board members are better able to communicate your successes to the community. To bring in a continual supply of new ideas each year, Van Dyke says, find a group of great volunteers and board members, changing them periodically to stay fresh.

Source: Michele Van Dyke, Executive Director, Luverne Area Community Foundation, Luverne, MN. Phone (507) 220-2424. E-mail: vandykem@sanfordhealth.org

Earmark Sufficient Time for Real Solicitation

How much real time do you devote to soliciting gifts? Thirty percent? Fifty percent?

Chances are it's less than you think.

The only actual time you can attribute to soliciting gifts is:

- Time spent meeting face to face with a prospect making the ask,
- Time it takes a prospect to read your appeal letter or e-mail request

for funds, and

- Time it takes to ask for a gift over the phone.

Everything else is important — research, cultivation, writing proposals — but it's not asking. Always be mindful of the actual time you, your colleagues and volunteers devote to inviting support for your nonprofit and its programs.

Goal Setting Should Be Ongoing

As important as it is to develop a yearly operational plan, complete with goals, quantifiable objectives, action plans and deadlines, planning shouldn't end there.

Monitor your goals and objectives weekly to map out and perhaps redefine what steps need to take place to stay on track in achieving your goals. It doesn't make sense to spend a good deal of time planning your year if you're not willing to monitor progress and make adjustments as needed.

Do Important Tasks First

Ever end your work day realizing you were so busy taking care of issues that kept coming up that you never got around to the tasks that mattered most? Here's a technique for putting important tasks ahead of daily "brush fires:"

1. At the end of your work day, list two or three tasks — those you can complete in an hour if given the time — for the following day.

2. When you arrive at work the next day, make a pledge that you will complete one or all of those tasks before moving on to anything else — including brush fires.

At the end of the day, regardless of what took place, you can take comfort in knowing you accomplished at least some of what mattered most. (Remember to jot down tomorrow's to do list before leaving for the day!)

DEVELOP A PLAN OF ACTION

Make Time to Develop an Annual Operational Plan

It's crucial to carry out thorough planning measures before jumping into a fundraising effort, especially if you're shooting for lofty goals.

A well-thought-out fundraising plan can break down those lofty goals into achievable components. Once yearly fundraising goals have been set, you're ready to begin mapping out a plan that will help achieve those goals.

Here is an example of steps to take to establish an annual operational plan:

1. **Set objectives** — Begin by coming up with a manageable number of quantifiable objectives that address overall goals. For example, if you have a yearly goal of raising $500,000 for your organization, you may have objectives that are similar to the following examples:

    * To secure $75,000 in $1,000-and-above gifts by fiscal year end.

    * To secure $40,000 in direct mail revenue by fiscal year end.

    * To secure $150,000 in phonathon gifts by fiscal year end.

    * To secure $40,000 through special fundraisers.

    * To secure $125,000 in corporate/foundation support by fiscal year end.

    * To secure $70,000 in new gifts from individuals and/or businesses.

2. **Action plans** — Once quantifiable objectives are set, formulate action plans that address how you intend to meet each objective. Action plans may outline special fundraising projects such as a special event or series of direct mail appeals or a phonathon. Collectively, the sum of each action plan will be equal to that total for a particular objective. Here are examples of action plans that address "securing $75,000 in $1,000-and-above gifts by fiscal year end:"

    * Make personal calls on all donors who gave at $1,000-plus level last year, inviting them to renew (or increase) giving for this fiscal year.

    * Host a president's reception in which all of last year's $1,000-plus contributors are invited and urged to bring a prospective donor who could give at that level.

    * Charge the development committee with responsibility for securing 10 or more new $1,000-plus gifts by year end.

    Although the above listed examples would require more detail — explaining what needs to happen when and who's in charge — you can see how each strategy supports how that particular objective will be achieved.

3. **Master calendar** — After all fundraising strategies for each objective have been spelled out through action plans, it's time to assemble a master timetable or calendar that includes the target date for every strategy and action plan component — everything from production schedules for printed communications to phonathon planning schedules and so forth.

Operational Plan Components

Goals:	More lofty — set the direction of the department or organization.
Objectives:	Quantifiable, more narrow — support the organization's goals.
Action plans:	Spell out how each quantifiable objective will be attained.
Master calendar:	Chronological dates of who does what and by when; highly detailed.

Plan Your Production Cycle

Whether you're planning an event or outlining the production schedule for a brochure, begin with the last part of your project and work backwards to establish the time needed for each portion of the project.

No Gift Support History? Develop A First-year Plan

If your organization is just getting started in fundraising or has little history of gift support, it's important to begin by developing a first-year plan. Then put it into writing.

Your written plan should identify what can reasonably be raised during the course of a year and how. Set specific goals for direct mail, special events, etc.

Once that's done, develop a one-page action plan for each area describing what will be done when and by whom.

Here are some examples of what a first-year fundraising plan might include:

* Conduct two direct mail appeals during the fiscal year, one in the fall and another in the spring.

* Coordinate a volunteer-driven phonathon to invite everyone in your community (or service area) to become a donor at any level.

* Organize a special event that reaches out to a particular segment of your community and nets $10,000 or more.

DEVELOP A PLAN OF ACTION

Calendar Keeps Fundraising on Track

Shelby Anderson, associate director of field fundraising, and Jennifer Legere, director of field fundraising, of MADD National Office (Irving, TX), wanted a way to keep development officers at local offices on track with fundraising, so they gave them the necessary tools.

They created a cultivation calendar:

- Each month has different tips and tasks to perform to keep in contact with potential donors.

- The supporters are ranked from A to C; A being the highest level of support, B being the middle and C being support on a smaller level.

- To keep in contact, chapters are encouraged to call, e-mail and visit potential supporters in person. The calendar lets them know when communication should happen and who should do it.

- For example, in one week e-mails should be sent to all of the C companies, an A company should get a personal visit by a board member and faxes should go out to all companies.

Anderson says the calendars really work and Legere says the proof is in the pudding, so to speak. Strong fundraising staffs really take advantage of the calendar and follow it.

Anderson and Legere have collected the calendar tips themselves over the years. They also encourage chapters to take mental notes about each company to personalize the fundraising potential and mark it on their calendars.

Source: Shelby Anderson, Associate Director of Field Fundraising, Jennifer Legere, Director of Field Fundraising, MADD National Office, Irving, TX. Phone (469) 420-4580. E-mail: Shelby.Anderson@madd.org

Make To-do Lists a Part of Your Everyday Routine

Do you get bogged down putting out daily brushfires only to find out by day's end that little of what you had initially hoped to accomplish got any of your attention?

This can easily happen to anyone involved with fundraising, especially if priorities aren't clearly marked out in advance.

If you haven't already done so, get into the habit of making a daily to-do list that includes appointments and those

projects that you deem as highest priority. Some people make their to-do lists at the end of the previous day (so they can come to work and hit the ground running). Others choose to make that the first item of business each day.

Whatever method you use (Outlook, some other software, a digital voice recorder or a simple 3 X 5-inch note card), and whatever time of day you choose to do it, get into the daily habit of making a to-do list.

> To-do List — April 13, 2009
>
> 8:15:   Staff mtg.
>
> 10:30:   Meet w/Doris Osborne, President, Osborne, Inc.
>
> 12:00:   Lunch w/board member Elmer Lindstrom
>
> _____   Set three appointments for next week
>
> _____   Finish Hartwell proposal
>
> _____   Update prospect tracking summary

Yearly Plan Needs Focus

Your development shop undoubtedly has a written plan identifying the year's objectives, what needs to happen by when, and who is responsible. Still, it's important for every team member to agree on what matters most. To accomplish this, create a primary focus that takes precedence over all other objectives. Examples:

✓ To increase by 10 percent the number of annual contributors of $1,000-plus.

✓ To increase the number of first-time contributors by 20 percent.

✓ To initiate strategies that generate more business community support.

✓ To produce and present more individualized funding proposals that will generate more major gifts.

Minimize Those Unscheduled Visits

- Next time an unwanted visitor comes walking in your door, stand and remain standing during the visit. You'll be signaling that you're busy and can't take time for a lengthy discussion.

- If an uninvited colleague says "Got a minute?", turn over a three-minute egg timer on your desk and say, "For you I have three minutes!"

- Shorten unwanted visits by escorting associates back to their office "on your way to do something."

DEVELOP A PLAN OF ACTION

Calculate Time Invested Against Total Dollar Returns

As you map out your fundraising year and create an operational plan complete with goals, objectives, action plans and timeline, it's helpful to analyze the time invested in each fundraising strategy against the dollar return for that effort. If, for instance, you discover that a direct mail appeal you sent out took minimal time but produced a significant return, you may decide to increase direct mail appeals in the upcoming year instead of spending time on a labor-intensive special event that had a marginal return.

Although there are other factors one needs to evaluate when planning upcoming development strategies

(e.g., project costs, etc.), time is a key issue based on limited development personnel. And while it may be challenging to estimate the time required to carry out a particular fundraising strategy from beginning to end, you will no doubt be able to calculate invested time to a reasonable degree. The key is to be consistent in the way in which you arrive at calculations — whether your are including support staff time, etc.

The chart below helps to illustrate how you might analyze each fundraising effort's invested time against its dollar return.

Content not available in this edition

Cut Down Phone Time

- Ask your secretary to say, "Susan is in a meeting but will be returning calls at 3 p.m. Will that work for you?" If that time won't work, have your assistant ask when the call could be returned.

- When making or taking a call, take care of business first by saying, "What can I do for you?" Save small talk for the end of the call, if time allows.

Goal Setting Tip

Whenever you begin the process of setting next year's development goals, think positive. Rather than say, "There's no way we can do that," think to yourself: "What would need to happen to achieve that increase?"

Yearly Plan Should Address Key Categories

Whenever you create your yearly operational plan, complete with goals, quantifiable fundraising objectives, action plans and a calendar of what happens when, be sure that it addresses key development categories.

Those may include:

- ❏ Direct mail
- ❏ Board giving
- ❏ Business/corporate gifts
- ❏ Gift clubs or levels
- ❏ Online gifts
- ❏ Planned gifts
- ❏ Foundation grants
- ❏ Retention strategies
- ❏ Community campaign
- ❏ Major gifts
- ❏ Special events
- ❏ Personal calls
- ❏ Acquisition strategies
- ❏ Fundraising publications/ communications
- ❏ Database and records management
- ❏ Development policies/ procedures
- ❏ Sponsorships
- ❏ Telesolicitation (phonathons)
- ❏ Organization giving (faith-based, etc.)
- ❏ Staff training
- ❏ Volunteer involvement
- ❏ Individual giving
- ❏ Donor stewardship

DEVELOP A PLAN OF ACTION

Strategies Define How You Plan to Achieve Objectives

If you have a list of quantifiable objectives you'd like to achieve in the coming year, a strategies list will help you develop a plan of action. Examples include:

❑ Increase the number of face-to-face solicitation calls to new prospects by ___ percent.

❑ Generate ___ more memorial and in-tribute gifts over last year.

❑ Develop three direct mail appeals aimed at nondonors.

❑ Create a wish list with the intent of generating ___ new contributors.

❑ Enlist a volunteer committee to make ___ calls per volunteer per month.

❑ Initiate a campaign among last year's donors to recruit a new contributor for the upcoming year.

❑ Invite board members to approach three new prospects for membership in the President's Order of Distinction.

❑ Expand an existing special event with the intent of building attendance by ___ new participants.

❑ Create a new special event with anticipated first year attendance of ___.

❑ Provide ___ presentations to civic groups with the intent of generating ___ new donors.

❑ Enlist one civic group to take on your organization as a yearlong service project and raise funds (and new donors) on your behalf.

The Master Calendar Is Your Plan's Centerpiece

An important and sometimes overlooked portion of the operational plan is that of the timetable or master calendar.

This important calendar makes up the final portion of an operational plan and should take into account all of the goals, objectives, strategies and action plans and bring together the dates for everything that is to occur throughout the coming year.

In addition to identifying what is to occur, the master calendar links planned actions to specific audiences and delineates who is ultimately responsible for carrying out each action.

Investing the time up front to craft a well-thought-out calendar will pay off throughout the year ahead. Well-planned master calendars help to organize complex activities during the year and allow staff to prepare for upcoming programs and events with much greater effectiveness.

Your operational plan and the accompanying master calendar should be an important part of regular staff meetings.

The example here represents an abbreviated version of a master calendar — that portion of your yearly operational plan that details what needs to happen when and by whom.

2009-10 Master Calendar

Date	Action/Event	Audience	Person(s) Responsible
1/4	Evaluate '08 Tour of Homes event		SP Committee
1/12	Board meeting	Board	Sissel
1/15-26	Draft Planned Gifts newsletter		Feldt
2/5	Planned Gifts newsletter to printer		Feldt
2/12	Send Planned Gifts newsletter	Planned Gifts List	Feldt
2/15	Quarterly Open House/Tour	Chamber of Commerce	Thompson
4/12	Board meeting	Board	Sissel
4/16	Tour of Homes planning meeting	Special Events Committee	Thompson
5/16	Quarterly Open House/Tour	Century Club Members	Thompson
5/20	Send Volunteer Picnic invitations	Previous Year's Volunteers	Thompson
6/12	Volunteer Picnic	Previous Year's Volunteers	Thompson
7/12-13	Board meeting and retreat	Board	Sissel
8/5-16	Develop & draft direct mail concept		Mitchell
8/15	Heritage Society Luncheon	Society Members	Feldt
8/15	Quarterly Open House/Tour	Planned Gift Prospects	Thompson/Feldt
8/26	Direct mail appeal to printer		
9/3-4	Strategic planning meeting	Key Individuals	Sissel/Mitchell
9/5	Direct mail appeal/ announce phonathon	Entire Mailing List Under $1,000	Mitchell
9/10	Tour of Homes planning meeting	Special Events Committee	Thompson
9/16-27	Draft Planned Gifts newsletter		Feldt
9/23	Send Appreciation Banquet invitations	$1,000+ Donors	
10/7	Planned Gifts newsletter to printer		Feldt
10/8	Tour of Homes planning meeting	Special Events Committee	Thompson
10/11	Board meeting	Board	Sissel
10/11	Appreciation Banquet	$1,000+ Donors	Sissel
10/14	Send Planned Gifts newsletter	Planned Gifts List	Feldt
10/14-17	Annual Phonathon	Past Donors (Under $1,000)	Thompson
10/20-24	Annual Phonathon	Nondonors	Thompson
11/11	Send Tour of Homes invitation	Last Year's Attendees/Others	Thompson
11/14	Quarterly Open House/Tour	Greater Sacramento Realtors	Thompson
12/2	Send holiday greeting	$100+ Donors/Board/Volunteers	Mitchell
12/2-7	Holiday Tour of Homes	Targeted by Committee & Invite	Thompson

Fundraising for Beginners: Essential Procedures for Getting a Fundraising Program Up and Running.
Edited by Scott C. Stevenson.
© 2009 Stevenson, Inc. Published 2009 by Stevenson, Inc.

DEFINE, DEVELOP AND MANAGE YOUR DATABASE

Your database or mailing list serves as the foundation from which you will work to cultivate relationships with both donors and would-be donors. It should include anyone who has any connection to your charity and those with whom you hope to establish relationships. Your database will allow you to connect targeted mailings and manage donor records. It serves as an ever-changing list, adding new names, updating information and, in some instances, removing records.

Spend Time Developing Your Mailing List

If your organization has little fundraising history, begin by developing a solid mailing list or database to solicit funds through direct mail appeals, personal calls and telesolicitation. List persons with current or past connection to your organization, such as:

- Clients/customers (e.g., past/present students, patients, members, attendees)
- Anyone who ever made a gift to your organization
- Volunteers; current/past employees; board members
- Local businesses (begin with chamber members)
- Other local nonprofit organizations
- Residents in ZIP codes around your service area

With the database in place, start strategizing ways to approach potential supporters.

Database Info

While you will eventually add more background information (e.g., linkage to charity, financial information, etc.), your initial mailing list should include these basic components:

- ✓ Prospect name
- ✓ Title
- ✓ Spouse
- ✓ Home address and phone
- ✓ Business address and phone
- ✓ E-mail addresses

Building a Mailing List From Scratch Or Build on an Existing One

Whether expanding an established mailing list or starting from scratch, it's important to selectively build your list if you hope to cultivate new and larger gifts. Begin by adding names of those persons who already contribute to or make use of your organization's services.

Here are some ways to capture names with giving potential:

1. Place a guest book in key locations frequented by visitors.

2. Have a fish bowl available for business cards — include a monthly drawing for a donated item.

3. Include a return postcard in mailings inviting new names to be added to your mailing list.

4. Review names of top donors to other organizations and add their names to your list.

5. Add all current, past and potential vendors.

6. Include current as well as past board members.

7. Include current and retired employees.

8. Don't forget the obvious: Those who have benefited from your services and perhaps relatives of former clients (e.g., students, patients, members).

9. Include active and past volunteers.

10. Selectively add residents of exclusive ZIP/postal codes.

11. Expand your list of major businesses and foundations.

Gather E-mail Addresses

Have you been collecting e-mail addresses of those on your regular mailing list? E-mail can be another means of cultivating constituents and provide another avenue for soliciting support. Another important benefit: No postage fees!

Collect the addresses by:

1. Sending a postcard to your entire mailing list inviting everyone to "send, fax, call or e-mail your e-mail addresses back to us."

2. Including a place for e-mail addresses on all pledge forms and other bounce backs.

3. When conducting phonathons, instruct callers to ask for e-mail addresses at the end of the call, when verifying the donor's address.

Build a Mailing List Of Qualified Names

If you have a mailing list of 1,000 quality names and get a 3 percent response rate, it makes sense to build your list — with quality names — even if the response rate drops somewhat.

One cost-effective alternative to building a donor base is to get names from board members, volunteers and current donors and send out personalized letters. Each board member, volunteer and donor could write a personal note on the letters that are being sent to people he/she knows. This procedure accomplishes another worthwhile objective as well: It gets your constituents involved in fund development, and their increased involvement may lead to increased giving.

DEFINE, DEVELOP AND MANAGE YOUR DATABASE

Turn to Those You Serve for Names

Want to build your mailing list? Turn to those you serve: students, graduates, former patients, members and others.

Invite those you serve, as well as those you have served in the past, to share the names of family, friends and associates with your organization.

To encourage them to add to your mailing list:

- **Invite referrals through direct mail.** Include bounce backs in all of your mailings. Send a special appeal that asks for a gift and names of potential donors. Include a P.S. on individual correspondence and e-mails.

- **Ask online.** Use your website to invite visitors to submit names to be added to your mailing list.

- **Take advantage of public gatherings.** Whenever you have an event, ask those present to fill out a referral card or share referral names with a staff person.

- **Don't overlook the use of premiums.** Consider offering inexpensive premiums to anyone who refers names: a free ticket to an event, discount coupons and more.

- **Ask for names during one-on-one meetings.** Whenever you call on a current contributor, don't leave without asking for a referral.

Call Reports Are More Than a Record

If you're new to development, a call report is a written summary of what was said during a meeting with a prospect or donor. A call report should always be completed following substantive communication with a prospect or donor. Persons who think the purpose behind a call report is simply to provide a record of what was said, however, are wrong. Although call reports do leave a lasting record of key conversation points, they should also accomplish other key aims. The completed call report should:

1. **Point out the primary objective of the call.** Was the visit intended to cultivate a prospect, solicit the prospect, introduce your organization to someone new or perhaps learn more about a prospect's funding interests? This key objective should be known prior to the visit and should be recorded as the first item on the call report.

2. **Illustrate the degree to which the caller accomplished the stated objective.** The summary of the visit should provide answers as to whether the objective was met.

3. **Make mention of next steps.** Follow-up is crucial to any prospect/donor communication. It's important to articulate follow-up steps after all key communications and include the time frame in which those steps should be completed (e.g., solicit gift within two weeks, deliver a proposal in 30 days, etc.) .

Update Lost Addresses

Part of good database management is keeping addresses as current as possible. But that's sometimes easier said than done with the mobility of today's society.

To help retrieve updated addresses for lost constituents:

- ❑ List lost constituents' names on your website with a link to an e-mail to send current contact information should the person being sought or someone who knows where he/she is reads it.

- ❑ Include lists of lost constituents in particular mailings, including an e-mail or toll-free number to contact with current information.

- ❑ Display names of lost constituents at your events along with a "Help us find these important folks!" note.

- ❑ Check with constituents' last known employers. If they won't share a current address, ask them to forward mail that asks for updated addresses.

CALL REPORT — XYZ CHARITY

Name of Prospect/Donor _____

Call Made By _____ Date of Call _____

Type of Call (Phone, personal visit, etc.) _____ Location _____

Primary Objective: _____

Summary of Call: _____

_____

_____

Next Steps/Deadline

1. _____

2. _____

3. _____

DEFINE, DEVELOP AND MANAGE YOUR DATABASE

Use Tracer Cards to Locate Lost Constituents

Keeping track of constituents is an important task of any fundraising organization. If you don't know where they are, you can't keep them informed about programs and can't solicit them for funds.

Tracer cards such as the one shown below are one method for locating lost constituents. If you are unable to locate a constituent, send the tracer cards to his/her relatives or last-known employers. Or mail them

to constituents to verify new addresses when you first learn of them.

In addition to making sure a home address is correct, ask the constituent for a new phone number, business address, e-mail address and other pertinent information. The cards are also appropriate to send to newly married or newly employed constituents, asking for updated names and addresses while also offering congratulations.

Sample Tracer Card

[Name of Nonprofit] is continuously updating the records of more than 30,000 individuals who have ties to our organization. This information is only for official use of [Name of Nonprofit].

We would appreciate your personal confirmation of the information on the reverse side of this card. Please indicate if our information is correct. If not, please make the necessary changes.

Additional information will be helpful for your personal biographical file.
Thank you for your help!

PLEASE RETURN TODAY!

Name _____
Home Address _____
City _____
Phone _____ State _____ ZIP _____
Preferred E-mail _____

☐ Single ☐ Married
Spouse: _____
Title _____
Business Address _____
City _____
Phone _____ State _____ ZIP _____
Website _____
☐ Please send update me on news at [Name of Nonprofit]

Include Businesses On Your Mailing List

■ Be sure to include your community's chamber membership on your mailing list and keep the membership list updated. These are civic-minded people — as evidenced by the fact that they pay chamber dues — and therefore, more likely to support philanthropic causes.

Build Your E-mail Database

E-mail has opened up an entirely new avenue of communication to use to introduce, cultivate, solicit and steward. Work to build your e-mail database at every touch point you have with prospects and donors: pledge forms, sign-up sheets, change-of-address forms, etc.

How Do You Define Your Solicitable Base?

What your solicitable base is depends on whether you define it as who is solicitable or who you decide to solicit, says Sarah Berger, annual fund director, The College of St. Catherine (St. Paul, MN).

Who is solicitable and who you decide to solicit are two different things, she says: "I believe you get into tricky territory if you eliminate those prospects who have not given for three years in order to increase your participation rate. It's different if you consider them solicitable but choose not to spend money soliciting them."

Berger says they solicit everyone. "It's amazing how long someone can be lapsed or be a non-donor and appear out of nowhere — often because life circumstances change or the college did something that made them proud so they show it with a contribution."

Think twice before excluding certain donors/prospects from your database because they haven't given in a few years, she says.

If you're experiencing poor response rates, ask yourself:

- Do we have good contact information for our prospects?
- How many times do we contact prospects before they make a gift? Berger says four to six contacts is ideal.
- Is the poor response rate new? Has something changed?
- Are we segmenting and personalizing enough?
- If we eliminate donors who haven't given for three years, what will be the long-term impact of that decision?

Source: Sarah Berger, Director of the Annual Fund, The College of St. Catherine, St. Paul, MN. Phone (651) 690-8840. E-mail: slberger@stkate.edu

DEFINE, DEVELOP AND MANAGE YOUR DATABASE

How to Build a Database of Qualified Prospects

The first question fundraisers need to ask when starting the process of building a database of qualified prospects is: Who cares about us and why?

"If an organization's mission statement is truly in sync with what the organization is doing, it provides a way to help identify who cares about it and why," says Tony Poderis, consultant.

Whether they are stewards of other people's money or individual contributors, people who are willing to give to an organization usually fall into one of two groups, says Poderis: those whose lives have been touched by the organization or those who are influenced and impressed by an organization's work or its leadership.

"Hospitals always put former patients high on their list of potential donors because their lives have been touched by the organization," he says. "Schools have entire departments devoted to alumni relations."

Every organization should have a database of its clients/users to prospect for donors, says Poderis, because even if the organization serves a clientele unlikely to be able to make gifts, those clients may lead to previously untapped sources. "When I worked for Big Brothers of Cleveland, which served more than 500 boys who did not have fathers at home, the mothers weren't able to give much money but a little research showed 10 percent of them worked at a utility company. When we pointed this out in our solicitation of the utility company and included endorsements from employees/mothers, we received gifts in excess of the company's usual. So, when it comes to finding donors: prospect, prospect, prospect and look for connections."

Poderis says viable prospects can be found by:

- Asking for names from your organization's board of trustees; suggestions from those already giving; and suggestions of new prospects from participants in prospect identification and rating

meetings who know the community and have money to give.
- Searching public resources (e.g., library, business publication, etc.), which have records of stock ownership, real estate holdings, salary data, business and career histories, family tree information, etc. of those with the means and history of giving money and who live and work in your service area.
- Gathering annual reports from similar organizations and reviewing their donor listings as potential donors to your cause.

Source: Tony Poderis, Consultant and Author, Willoughby Hills, OH. Phone (440) 944-9230. E-mail: tony@raise-funds.com

Records Management Tip

Trying to determine if someone in your database has passed away? You will find any of these sites to be helpful:

www.legacy.com — Nationwide resource for obituaries.

www.ancestry.com — Family history records on the Internet.

www.rootsweb.com — Free genealogy website.

Maintain a Summary Sheet in Each Donor File

How many times have you gone to a prospect's or donor's file seeking one piece of information and having to look through the entire file to locate it?

While many nonprofits have sophisticated computer software to record donor information, there will always be a place for the traditional filing system as a way of maintaining information that 1) may be too cumbersome for computer records, and, 2) serves as an important backup in the event of a computer crash.

To help reduce file review time, attach a contact information sheet inside the cover of each prospect/donor file.

All too often important data is lost because there's no easy way to capture it, or staff turns over and it's gone forever. The contact sheet provides an easy way to summarize visits and correspondence with prospects over a period of time.

Summary sheets can also keep a running total of gifts made along with the purpose of each gift and a corresponding gift acknowledgment date.

Contact Information

CONTACT NAME/ADDRESS		PHONE/FAX
DATE	ACTION	

BUILD BOARD SUPPORT

Your goal should be to build a financially capable board of givers and getters. Their level of support will set the bar for gifts that follow, so it's vital that you take a long-term approach in identifying, qualifying, enlisting and nurturing board members who are committed to your fundraising efforts.

Retreat Helps Board Understand Its Role

Utilize board retreats to nurture members' interest and involvement in fund development.

At the Girl Scout Council of Orange County (Costa Mesa, CA) annual board retreat, Kathleen O'Neill, senior director of development and marketing, led a discussion on how the board can help strengthen the culture of philanthropy within the organization and provided an overview of the major gifts process. Half of the four-hour retreat was dedicated to the discussion and overview of the board's role in fundraising and the major gifts process.

The fund development discussion began with a brief talk by a business leader serving on a very successful and sophisticated fundraising board. "We thought by having a colleague who is a peer talk about that board and its successes, it would provide a wonderful example and raise the awareness and understanding within our board," says O'Neill.

The remainder of the discussion consisted of the development and major gift processes. "We wanted to educate them about the development process," says O'Neill. "We got them on an even footing in terms of fundraising and where the organization stands.

"They understood their role could be what they're comfortable with and the different types of solicitation methods and how they could impact and become involved in the different levels of the fund development pyramid," says O'Neill. "They began to see what they could do personally and that it wasn't intimidating."

Source: Kathleen O'Neill, Senior Director of Development and Marketing, Girl Scout Council of Orange County, Costa Mesa, CA. Phone (714) 979-7900. E-mail: koneill@gscoc.org

Fund Development Should Be a Part of Board Orientation

Every new board member should benefit in some way from a board orientation session. In fact, you may consider inviting veteran board members to attend the session, if they'd like to do so.

Be sure to devote sufficient time to the development department's programs during that orientation gathering. Use that time to bring board members up to speed on various aspects of your fundraising efforts.

Here's a sampling of some of the topics you might choose to cover:

1. Introduction to and review of individual staff responsibilities.

2. Review of the board's development responsibilities and expectations.

3. An explanation of your reporting system for gifts.

4. A review of current fundraising procedures and policies.

5. A period of discussion on ways board members can further fund-raising efforts.

6. Demonstrations on cultivation and solicitation techniques.

7. A review of current funding opportunities.

8. An historical review of the organization's fundraising efforts.

One Board Member Needs to Set Precedent

You can have a "who's who" of individuals on your board of trustees, but until one steps forward with an unprecedented, sacrificial gift, others may very well refrain from giving at highly capable levels.

Work at convincing that most capable board member of his/her role before other board members step up to the plate with less-than-desirable pledges. Help that single board member realize the potential he/she possesses.

Paint a picture of what could be versus what's probable without that level of leadership. Your shared vision should depict specific examples of how your organization will achieve greatness with a great gift.

Set Annual Goal For Board Gifts

If your organization has little history of fundraising, be sure to set an annual goal for board gifts. Without it, you will find it challenging, if not impossible, to raise the bar in terms of giving in subsequent years.

Have your board's development committee come up with a realistic yet challenging goal for annual board support. Point out that the board's level of annual support sets a precedent for others who give. Many nonprofit boards will even approve a minimum gift level that board members are expected to give (or get) on an annual basis.

When you share a written report of total gifts to date (for the year) at board meetings, include a separate line item that reflects board gifts to date in relation to the board's giving goal.

BUILD BOARD SUPPORT

Use Board Meetings to Rally Enthusiasm

Don't use regular board meetings simply to report dull gift statistics. Instead, approach them as opportunities to build enthusiasm and support for your fundraising objectives.

Although you may meet one on one with individual board members from time to time, board meetings represent the single best opportunity for collectively cultivating and persuading members to buy into your plans. Consider some of these ideas as you prepare for your next board meeting:

- Select four or five similar agencies that have achieved superior fund-raising success and use them as models to build board enthusiasm.

- Invite a recent major donor (nonboard member) to attend the next meeting and tell the board what inspired him/her to make a significant gift to your cause.

- Conduct a brainstorming exercise with board members to discuss what it would take to generate a history-making gift for your organization. What would have to change in order for that to happen?

- Assemble a panel of those served by your institution (e.g., students, youth, former patients) to discuss — in the board's presence — why they think your charity is worthy of major gifts.

- Invite a foundation officer to tell board members what it takes to merit the foundation's financial support.

- Share a massive list of your community's nondonors with the board and ask them what it would take to convert a percentage of those named to donor status.

When You're New to the Job: Get to Know Your Board Members

If you've just accepted a position as chief fundraiser for an organization, one of the first and best uses of your time is to introduce yourself to each board member.

Not only is it important that they meet you, it's equally important for you to learn more about them and analyze what most matters to them. If these persons are responsible for setting a standard of giving for your cause, you should study their history of involvement and potential for support.

Take the time to review each board member's file and chat with other staff in the know before setting individual appointments. Then, when the opportunity to meet one on one takes place, do your best to cover the following points:

1. Ask the board member to share what he/she considers the organization's greatest strengths and shortcomings.

2. Find out what excites the board member most about your cause (possible clues to his/her funding interests).

3. Get a read on the board member's perception of past gift support and the potential for future support. Ask what he/she considers as future funding priorities.

4. Ask the board member to tell you about him/herself. There may be no better time to invite a board member to share such personal information than now, since you are new and it is appropriate to ask such a question.

Whether your organization has five or 30 board members, taking the time to meet one on one with these individuals will provide a wealth of knowledge as you go about the task of shaping future fund development plans.

Identify and Prioritize Affluent Board Considerations

Regardless at what level your charity chooses to define a major gift, your board members should comprise a significant percentage of the major gift prospect pool. It's not uncommon to have collective board member contributions account for as much as 30 to 60 percent of a capital campaign's lead gifts.

To help steer your board nominations committee in the right direction, take steps to ensure those being considered as board nominees have the potential for major gifts:

1. Sell your nominations committee on the importance of board affluence. Convince this group that major gifts can only be realized if board members set the pace.

2. Develop a file of affluent individuals' names to share with your nominations committee. Who among your existing constituency has achieved or has the potential for exemplary giving? Also, look at names of those giving major gifts to other organizations.

3. Take action only on those names submitted for consideration at an earlier nomination committee meeting. This allows time for both staff and board members to conduct any background research that will shed more light on the candidates' financial capability and inclination to give.

BUILD BOARD SUPPORT

Report Encourages Increased Board Member Support

A monthly report to the development committee of the Associated Early Care and Education, Inc. (Boston, MA) compares unrestricted, temporarily restricted and permanently restricted contributions made in the prior fiscal year with those made in the current fiscal year by individuals (board, employees, individuals and volunteers), corporations and foundations.

Development officials update the contributors report on the last day of each month and distribute it to members of the board's development committee.

The purpose of the report is threefold, says Shaké Sulikyan, associate director:

1. To keep the development committee up to date on fundraising progress;

2. To encourage development committee (and board at large) members to get more involved with fundraising, as opposed to just advising the department; and

3. To encourage board members to give/step up their own giving.

"The report has helped us evaluate our board giving program and was useful in convincing the board chair to send out a special appeal to the board (which went out in March and was fairly successful)," she says.

In addition, Sulikyan says: "The monthly report has also helped us compare the current fiscal year to last year, allowing us to analyze trends in giving; provided the development committee with a detailed yet summarized way to look at information; sparked committee discussion about stepping up our individual giving efforts and helped committee co-chairs in reporting our goals and progress to the board at large."

Source: Shaké Sulikyan, Associate Director, Associated Early Care and Education, Inc., Boston, MA. Phone (617) 695-0700, ext. 274. E-mail: ssulikyan@ associatedearlycareandeducation.org

Share Fundraising Efforts at Each Board Meeting

If your organization doesn't have much history at raising funds, be sure to provide your board with a written and oral report at all regularly scheduled board meetings. This both informs them about what's going on and helps them to own your development efforts.

Share a standard report of gifts to date for the current fiscal year, and break down the sources of those gifts (i.e., businesses, individuals, employees, etc.) in relation to goals. Additionally, summarize fundraising projects that will occur between now and the next board meeting, inviting board members to take an active role in particular aspects.

Officials with Boston's Associated Early Care and Education, Inc. provide this monthly report to their development committee to compare giving from one fiscal year to the next.

Content not available in this edition

BUILD BOARD SUPPORT

Nurture Board Productivity

A common complaint among nonprofit workers is that their board isn't fully engaged in fundraising efforts. Likewise, board members complain about not being fully utilized.

So how do you bridge that gap and get your board "on board"?

Make specific requests of board members rather than just asking them to help in general terms, advises Dana Kindrick, executive administrative assistant, Navarro College Foundation (Corsicana, TX).

Tying board members to specific projects allows them to make their own best contribution. The following tips can help:

❑ **Know your board.** Every member should have a defined purpose prior to being asked to sit on a board. An attorney may help rewrite by-laws. A financial planner may help with planned gifts. Without defined roles, it's hard for board members to be effective.

❑ **Really know your board.** Fully vet your prospective board members. Don't be afraid to ask specifics about how many hours per month they can donate, what relationships they have that may be valuable to your cause and what role(s) they see themselves taking. This will not scare off true prospects, and if it does, you're better off with that happening now rather than halfway through your capital campaign.

❑ **Make sure they know you.** Be clear about expectations before a prospective member accepts your offer. Have a job description, guidelines for minimum board gifts and expected time commitment to help them make an informed decision.

❑ **Do an annual needs assessment for your board.** When you formally evaluate your board, you might be surprised to find you have four attorneys, but no financial planners. You might have a board full of people donating their own money, but are uncomfortable asking others to donate. An honest evaluation will help you right those situations for a more balanced and productive board.

Source: Dana Kindrick, Executive Administrative Assistant, Navarro College Foundation, Corsicana, TX. Phone (903) 875-7591. E-mail: dana.kindrick@navarrocollege.edu

Get Your Board To Assume Annual Gift Responsibility

It's not uncommon for boards to think "it's the responsibility of staff to meet annual fund goals." That's wrong. Board members should feel some sense of ownership for meeting and exceeding annual gift goals.

Engage your board in annual giving by getting them to approve some portion of your annual giving goal. Depending on your board's size and level of past involvement, convince the board development committee to accept responsibility and seek full board approval for any of these yearly goals:

✓ To secure [X] number of gifts throughout the fiscal year within a defined gift range (e.g., $500 and above).

✓ To individually sell so many special event tickets each year.

✓ To individually contribute a minimum amount to the annual fund each year.

✓ To individually make a minimum number of new prospect solicitation calls.

Use Peer-to-peer Calls for Board Members

How do you go about inviting board members to support your annual fund on a yearly basis? Do you treat them differently than other donors?

Here's one way to go about maximizing annual gifts from individual board members:

1. Along with your CEO, approach your board's most sacrificial donor — the individual who gives the most each year based on his/her financial ability. After soliciting him/her for this year's gift, ask that individual to approach your board chair and three other of your most generous donors.

2. In addition to soliciting the board chair and three other board members for support, ask each of them to approach three additional board members — using a staff person, your CEO or another board member as a team solicitor.

Use this pyramid approach to stress your key message (regarding board support) and establish a board tradition of peer-to-peer solicitation.

Board Involvement Tip

■ To get your board more involved in fund development, invite individual board members to accompany you on stewardship calls to thank donors who recently made gifts at higher levels. Board members will be energized by the experience and become more inclined to accompany you on future solicitation calls. Bonus: Donors will appreciate having a board member along to say thanks.

POSITION YOURSELF FOR SOLICITATION SUCCESS

There are but three ways you can ask for gift support: written communications, phone and face-to-face visits. Clearly, face-to-face contacts will produce the greatest success, so it's important to prioritize prospects to ensure top prospects merit those personal contacts. This chapter will provide you with some basic tools and ideas to position you for solicitation success.

Just Getting Started? Find Yourself One or More Mentors

New to the fundraising profession? One of the smartest moves you can make is to identify one to three individuals who can share their wisdom and experience. But don't go to just anyone — seek the counsel of those who have:

1. **Experienced it all.** Turn to those who have been in the profession for 10 or more years. They have seen many changes in the profession and have no doubt overcome many challenges during that time.

2. **Achieved a record of success.** Talk's cheap. Demonstrated success takes time and hard work. Recognize what they

have accomplished and the responsibilities they have held before approaching them for help.

3. **Demonstrated a willingness to be your mentor.** Building a mentor relationship takes time. Be sure those you have identified have the patience and interest to share their insight.

4. **Exemplified those values that deserve your admiration.** Do they first look out for the welfare of those on whom they're calling? Do they adhere to prescribed professional ethics such as those set forth by The Association of Fundraising Professionals (www.afpnet.org)?

Start by Evaluating Existing Programs

As you work to prepare an operational plan for the upcoming year — a plan that identifies goals, objectives, strategies, action plans and timetables — it's critical that you begin by evaluating what is currently being done and making changes based on the success (or lack of success) of existing programs.

As a first step in the planning process, it will be enormously helpful if you can evaluate the current year in light of past years' results. Examples of historical review may include:

- Total gifts received each year
- Yearly gift types — annual, planned and so on
- Giving by constituency type
- Numbers of contributors by category

As you evaluate the existing year's programs in light of previous year's

results, when possible, attempt to quantify each program in terms of: net gift revenue, the cost-to-revenue ratio, the percentage of staff time and budget required to carry out the program and a comparison to other programs.

In addition, weigh each program in light of its long- versus short-term payoff. A planned gifts program, for instance, may take years to achieve results, however those results may far outweigh another program's benefits.

Examples of individual programs to be evaluated include:

- Direct mail appeals
- Personal solicitation calls
- Telemarketing programs
- Special events
- Annual and planned gift programs

These program evaluation results will serve as your planning foundation.

If You're New To the Job...

If you're relatively new to your position, approach your nonprofit's board members about individually escorting you around the community and introducing you to its movers and shakers. It's not only a great way to be introduced, it's also a great way to establish rapport with board members and involve them in fund development.

Make Use Of a Tickler System

Good development practices require proper cultivation of large numbers of people. Proper cultivation requires attention to detail.

Do you have a tickler system in place for remembering donors' and prospects' birthdays and anniversaries? Are you prepared to call on donors at the appropriate time to thank them for their past support? Have you identified the application deadlines for various foundations?

Whether you create and manage it or someone else does it for you, a tickler system of key dates will ensure you are staying on top of details that require your attention.

Use a tickler system for:

- Donor/prospect birthdays
- Donor/prospect anniversaries
- Foundation application deadlines
- Direct mail appeal drop dates
- Drop dates for other key mailings
- Key public events
- Regularly scheduled meetings
- Thank-you calls on key donors
- Phone calls to select donors/prospects

POSITION YOURSELF FOR SOLICITATION SUCCESS

Enlist 100 Businesses at $100 Each

If your organization has little history of fundraising, it's important to begin to build a broad base of support that, hopefully, turns into repeat giving. One yearlong strategy is to enlist 100 business contributors who each give $100 (or more) with the expectation that they will begin contributing annually. (The number of businesses and dollar goal may differ depending on your community's size and the philanthropic environment.)

To implement this "100 business donors at $100 each" strategy:

1. Enlist a group of current business supporters who will agree to call on businesses on your behalf.

2. Develop a packet of materials volunteers (and you) can use to market $100-plus annual gifts.

3. Hold a series of small-group receptions at your facility or elsewhere as a means of telling your story to business attendees.

4. Coordinate a special event — golf classics are common examples — aimed at the business community with an entry fee of $100.

5. Conduct a phonathon on businesses using a funding project appealing to them.

6. Carry out at least two direct mail appeals during the year aimed at members of the business community.

Starting a Development Program From Scratch

Is your charity overly reliant on government support?

When officials with The MIND Institute (Albuquerque, NM) found their government funding would end in 2008, they realized they had a lot of work to do. The organization had never done any fundraising, had no donor database, and its staff, including Executive Director Kathy Burrows, had no fundraising experience.

"We didn't even know enough about ourselves and fundraising to be able to tell consultants what we wanted them to do," says Burrows. And since their funding came from the government, they couldn't use existing funds to hire a consultant for fundraising purposes. "We had to get an outside source for seed money to start the process," she says.

So Burrows began educating herself about fund development. She spent a day at the Association of Fundraising Professionals (AFP) talking to consultants who did fund development start-up. She met with organizations similar to hers with a track record of success to learn what they were doing right. She attended fundraising seminars.

For help writing a request for proposals for hiring a consultant, Burrows turned to the Minnesota Medical Foundation. Officials there helped her write a proposal that would attract consultants interested in helping within her organization's $50,000 budget, and she was able to recently hire a consultant. "The foundation helped us create a realistic goal for what the consultant could do for what we could spend," she says.

MIND officials have just started to put their fundraising program together and to determine what to do first, Burrows says. Their first step has been to educate board members about the fundraising process. "I talk to board members during meetings about fundraising and what it entails," she says. The consultant they hired also presented at the board meeting about the objectives of the first phase.

"We've found that it has been easier to get board members involved in development if we can tell them what they need to do and why," says Burrows.

Source: Kathy Burrows, Executive Director, The MIND Institute, Albuquerque, NM. Phone (505) 272-7578. E-mail: kburrows@unm.edu

Rule of Thumb

- As a guide in annual giving, you can expect that roughly 65 percent of your total annual fund is made possible by 15 percent to 20 percent of your constituency.

Renew: It's Less Costly Than New

- Generally speaking, it costs four times the money and time to get a new gift as it does to renew one. Keep that fact in mind as you weigh the time you spend attracting new contributors versus time spent attempting to get past ones to give again.

Build on Existing Programs Before Starting New Ones

Sometimes development professionals are so overwhelmed by the pressure to increase gift support that they tend to focus on creating new fundraising strategies when what they should do is to build on existing programs that have shown past success.

One development shop, for instance, may decide to initiate a new special event instead of focusing on ways to expand their existing (and successful) $1,000-plus giving club membership. Additionally, when one diverts attention away from an existing program to begin a new effort, the existing program can easily fall short of expectations.

Examine how you can generate new and/or increased gifts by building on existing fundraising programs before leaping to a new and perhaps riskier approach.

POSITION YOURSELF FOR SOLICITATION SUCCESS

Getting Started When There's No History of Giving

The number of small charities interested in fundraising is growing rapidly.

If your organization has little or no history of generating gift revenue, the time couldn't be better to establish a development program. But if your charity is like many just getting into fundraising, the entire responsibility probably rests with one individual.

Here's your recipe for getting a fundraising program up and running:

- **Put it all in writing.** Develop a yearlong written plan. Even if it's only one page, draft an operational plan that lists fundraising goals for the year and breaks those goals down into quantifiable objectives. Include a master calender that identifies every step that will occur throughout the year to reach your objectives.

- **Assemble a core committee of determined volunteers.** Ask a handful of individuals who believe in your cause and have volunteer (or sales) experience to help you with fund development. Their job is to help identify, research, cultivate and solicit gifts. Be up front about the focus of their work.

- **Assemble a mailing list along with a series of direct mail appeals.** Include persons already connected to your charity in some way — employees, clients, board members, friends and volunteers. Review other charities' annual contribution lists; who among them should be included on your list? Once your list is assembled, plan for no fewer than two mailings during the course of your fiscal year that ask for gifts for a specific project.

- **Market an annual gifts (or membership) program.** Collect annual gifts literature from other nonprofits. Evaluate what it says and how they delineate giving levels and accompanying donor benefits. Then create an annual fund (or membership) brochure of your own.

- **Secure a three-year challenge.** Who among those you know would have both the ability and interest to make a challenge gift — preferably over a three-year period — that would match any new or increase gifts to your charity? A challenge gift will result in your first major gift and help to leverage other new and increased gifts from others.

- **Schedule regular face-to-face calls.** Make weekly face-to-face calls a high priority. Call on businesses/individuals on your own, and get your volunteers started making calls as well. After making sufficient calls with each volunteer — to train them — pair them up to begin making calls as teams.

- **Coordinate a distinctive special event.** With the assistance of an additional group of volunteers, initiate an annual special event as a way of attracting new supporters, generating additional gift revenue and getting your charity's story out to the public. Cover the event's costs by getting businesses to sponsor it.

Evaluate your progress toward goals monthly and make adjustments as needed. Celebrate victories along the way. Use your first year's success as a springboard for increasing your development budget, considering the addition of personnel and increasing next year's totals.

Make Time to Review Systems and Policies

As you work to develop efficiencies that generate additional gift support, increase the number of contributors, enhance your organization's image and more, it's important to examine existing systems and policies to be sure they are efficient, effective and meeting stewardship goals.

Here are a few examples of systems and policies you should examine yearly:

- Gift acknowledgment process
- Filing system
- Gift acceptance policy and procedures
- Planned gifts policy
- Endowment policies
- Job descriptions and responsibilities
- Prospect research policy
- Organizational structure
- Volunteer structure and committees
- Board structure and committees
- Memorial gifts program
- Prospect tracking systems
- Campaign structure and process
- Existing marketing materials
- Pledge forms, letters of intent, etc.
- Gifts-in-kind policy
- Database management procedures
- Board and volunteer training
- Professional development
- Board and volunteer selection
- Hiring procedures

POSITION YOURSELF FOR SOLICITATION SUCCESS

Maintain Contact With Your Predecessor

It's not uncommon for someone who is new to a job to never have contact with the person who occupied that same position before. The predecessor leaves his/her position, the new person is hired and, at best, is left with some notes and files from the former individual. It's a mistake not to attempt to make contact with the former employee to learn more about how he/she operated and to use that person as a resource.

Whether by phone, e-mail or face-to-face meetings, here's some of what can be reviewed with your predecessor over time:

- History about prospects, donors and board members that may not be apparent in files and call reports.

- Timing about certain events and procedures that isn't spelled out any place.
- Answers about your supervisor's management style and priorities.
- Insight into work habits and personalities of employees you are expected to manage.
- Further explanation about existing policies and development shop procedures.

Take the initiative to stay in touch with your predecessor. He/she will be honored that you seek his/her counsel. Plus, you'll be more likely to maintain that person's financial support of your organization if you demonstrate your openness to his/her advice.

Assemble a Can-do Committee of Willing Volunteers

It takes time to assemble and train a group of volunteers committed to fund development and willing to assist in the identification, cultivation, solicitation and stewardship of prospects and donors. But it's time well spent if you attract the right individuals and give them the nurturing they deserve.

If you're just getting started, begin by mapping out a yearlong plan that includes recruiting a small handful of volunteers. Agree to meet once a month, using your meetings to:

1) train and educate, and
2) review prospect names and assign calls.

In the beginning, accompany each volunteer on three or four calls so he/she can learn from your example and you can critique his/her presentation skills. After sufficient training, encourage the volunteers to pair up and make calls together or on their own.

Use Response Cards With Direct Mail, Face-to-face Calls

Every face-to-face or direct mail contact you have with people should allow you to invite their involvement with your organization in some capacity. Whether meeting with a first-time or long-time donor, the individual's growing involvement with your institution is the single most important factor in generating new or increased gifts, needed volunteer assistance, or both.

So what systems do you have in place that help to show you when someone may be interested? How do you know when someone might want to establish a scholarship? How do you know someone wants to get involved in planning a special event? When someone is willing to assist in your capital campaign?

The use of response cards or bounce backs should be incorporated whenever and wherever possible. Whenever a new brochure is developed, include an accompanying response card. Whenever correspondence is sent,

include a response card. Whenever you meet with anyone, select a response card that best fits the circumstances and share it with the prospect.

The response card gives others a tangible reason to get back to you. And when they do, you don't have to guess or read minds. You have evidence that they have expressed interest in learning more about your organization and perhaps, how they can assist your efforts.

As you can see from the example here, there is no limit on the number of ways in which you can use this simple tool. Assess the many ways in which bounce backs may be useful in your work.

Pleased to meet you.... Let's get to know each other.

Name _____
Address _____
City _____ State _____ ZIP _____
Daytime Phone _____
Evening Phone _____
Occupation_____ Title _____

I'm interested in learning more about the following:

- ❑ The college's history and mission.
- ❑ Distinguishing achievements of the college.
- ❑ Course offerings/majors.
- ❑ Career advising.
- ❑ Financial aid/scholarship assistance.
- ❑ Upcoming calendar of events.
- ❑ Speakers bureau topics.
- ❑ Volunteer opportunities.
- ❑ Exploring planned gift opportunities.
- ❑ Annual fund opportunities.
- ❑ Endowed gift opportunities.
- ❑ How to establish a scholarship.
- ❑ The college's future plans.
- ❑ Alumni activities and involvement.
- ❑ Distinguished graduates of the institution.
- ❑ Status of the endowment.
- ❑ Other _____

PROFITABLE DIRECT MAIL IDEAS

Properly planned and orchestrated, direct mail appeals can play a significant role in achieving success. They can also fail miserably if poorly planned. They can serve to generate first-time gifts and to renew past donors' support. They can be directed to targeted groups, and they can be conducted several times throughout the year. Most importantly, each direct mail appeal needs to carry a compelling message, one that calls people to action.

Map Out Yearly Direct Mail Appeals

To maximize gift revenue returns from direct mail, plan a year's worth of appeals in advance.

Using historical data, schedule a year's worth of appeals aimed at particular segments of your database (past contributors, non-donors, affinity groups, etc.), inviting support for particular funding projects.

There may be instances when an appeal is directed to your entire mailing list and others restricted to one or more segments of your database. Funding projects may vary from appeal to appeal as well.

Having a yearly schedule of appeals, such as the example shown here, helps to visualize the big picture and spot potential problems or missed opportunities. You may even choose to include other types of mailings (e.g., newsletters, invitations, announcements) in your schedule to visualize how various mailings play off one another.

2009 APPEALS SCHEDULE

Date	Audience	Size	Project	Comments
1/15	Past Contributors	2,234	Operations	
3/1	Past Contributors	2,234	Operations	Follow up: Non-responders
4/15	Area Businesses	3,040	Sponsorships	Multiple choices
6/12	Non-donors	6,466	Three projects	Multiple choices
9/15	Planned Gift Prospects	883	Planned gift invite	Includes bounce back
11/15	Lybunt Appeal	2,234	Operations	Follow up: Non-responders
12/1	Entire Database	8,700	Holiday Wish List	Multiple choices

Secure Sponsors to Underwrite Direct Mail Appeals

Does your organization have multiple direct mail appeals throughout the year?

If so, why not get local businesses or individuals to sponsor individual appeals or your entire annual package of mailings?

By encouraging a business or individual(s) to sponsor an appeal — underwriting its total cost with a gift — you can accomplish several objectives:

- To allow the sponsoring donor to see exactly how his/her gift is being used — in this case, to generate more money for the organization.

- To provide the sponsor with added visibility: "This mailing underwritten by..."

- To save needed budget dollars for other worthwhile programs.

- To allow greater financial flexibility in creating an attention-getting appeal.

Direct Mail Tips

1. If your goal is to build your donor base, ask for small gifts from new prospects.

2. Regularly share a wish list of fundable items that donors' gifts will make possible.

3. Use matching challenge gifts to increase your appeal's response rate.

Ideas for Expanding Your Donor Base

To build your donor list, make a commitment to send direct mail appeals to nondonors at least three times during the fiscal year. For each mailing, try a different approach to see what produces the best results.

Here are some choices to consider for each of your mailings to nondonors:

1. Secure a challenge gift in which the donor will match all first-time gifts from new donors. Direct the funds to a tangible project (e.g., a building addition that will enhance your services or a new program that will aid the needy) so donors will know and see how their gifts are being used.

2. Send nondonors a wish list of items they may wish to partially or totally fund. Include a variety of projects and accompanying gift amounts.

3. Conduct an appeal that asks everyone for the same modest gift, say $35, to be used for an appealing funding project — purchase a tree, pay one week's meals for the homeless, cover one day of camp expenses for youth, etc.

PROFITABLE DIRECT MAIL IDEAS

Personalized Message Makes for Direct Mail Appeal Success

An appeal with a simple tagline, "Then, Now and Again," has yielded the best results in direct mail campaign history for the Hebrew Academy of Tidewater/Strelitz Early Childhood Center (Virginia Beach, VA).

Eilene Rosenblum, director of development, says each piece of the direct mail appeal is a four-fold, 5 1/2 X 9-inch brochure featuring a school year photo of a donor juxtaposed with a present family photo (where the children are the current students).

A quote from the donor expressing gratitude for life lessons learned at the academy is featured under the family photo, with information on his/her subsequent education.

The brochure's next two pages feature text on the school's mission and need for financial support, mixed with photos of students who attend the K-6 and preschool division.

Mailed in three parts — August, December and April — the direct mail appeal was sent to 3,000 donors and prospective donors.

Unlike past years when donors who contributed after the first mailing were not sent additional mailings, Rosenblum says all 3,000 persons on the list received all three mailings, plus a thank-you note if they donated, so they could see the complete campaign.

This tactic — along with the use of former students at the center of the appeal's message — proved a winning combination, bringing in 500 gifts totaling more than $350,000. The average gift was $500 and the largest, $2,500.

"This approach yielded the best results for a direct mail appeal we have ever produced," says Rosenblum, pointing to the $50,000 increase in gifts over the prior year's annual campaign. "The personalized appeal resonated with recipients not only because they recognized themselves, but because they recognized their contemporaries. It also resonated with older people who saw their children or their children's children following in their footsteps."

Rosenblum says the mailing was such a success she is using it again for the upcoming year, featuring new participants and their families.

Source: Eilene Rosenblum, Director of Development, Hebrew Academy of Tidewater/Strelitz Early Childhood Center, Virginia Beach, VA. Phone (757) 424-4327. E-mail: Ehrosenblum@hebrewacademy.net

Juxtaposing a past class picture with the student today proved successful for a direct mail appeal for the Hebrew Academy of Tidewater/Strelitz Early Childhood Center (Virginia Beach, VA):

> *"The personalized appeal resonated with recipients not only because they recognized themselves, but because they recognized their contemporaries."*

Measure Your Direct Mail ROI

How do you calculate the ROI (return on investment) each time you send an appeal letter to a group of would-be contributors?

While there may be a number of factors you could consider (e.g., average size gift, total gifts raised, number of first-time gifts), the ROI is generally the number generated by dividing total profit of the mailing by the mailing's total cost.

Here are a few ways of calculating ROI:

A. Number of pieces mailed multiplied by:

B. Percent response rate multiplied by:

C. Average gift amount multiplied by:

D. Percentage of profit per gift.

E. Subtract this amount from total cost of the mailing for your ROI.

Content not available in this edition

PROFITABLE DIRECT MAIL IDEAS

Completing the Direct Mail Package

Those materials that accompany your appeal letter — the pledge card, brochure, return envelope and so on — are also important to your overall package. How these pieces complement one another and convey messages all contribute to the effectiveness of the effort.

Here are pointers regarding the extras which make up your appeal package:

1. Supporting materials in your package should reinforce your letter's message.

2. Develop a reply or pledge card that stands on its own. Readers will be more likely to misplace or toss your letter than the reply card.

3. Offer more than one payment option — credit card, monthly or quarterly payments.

4. If you incorporate a photo, include a caption or identify the individual.

5. Make your package easy to read by selecting a type font that is large enough and easily readable — factors important for senior citizens.

6. Before your package is printed, have more than one individual proof each piece.

7. Include your organization's phone and fax numbers on all printed materials. If online pledging is an option, list the website, and make sure it's up and running before your mailing is received.

8. Have someone unfamiliar with your organization read the entire package to spot unanswered questions and identify inconsistencies.

9. Your package design should promote your message, not confuse it.

10. Clearly delineate each giving level and its associated benefits.

11. Offer a special incentive for those who respond by a due date.

12. Print "address correction requested" on all appeals to help increase contacts.

13. Test the use of calendar giving envelopes with a portion of your constituency — one mailing includes 12 envelopes and encourages prospects to make monthly contributions.

14. Give your package the dummy test: Ask someone to open your mailing and express their reactions as they go through it. Observe how they open it and consider if your piece could be put together more effectively.

15. Keep paragraphs and sentences short to ensure ease of reading.

16. Ask a respected colleague to read your completed letter (and accompanying materials) to review its impact, flow and grammar.

17. If time permits, set your draft aside for a few days and then read it again.

Nine Ways to Improve Direct Mail Appeals

With all of the competition for philanthropic dollars, appeal letters not only need to grab the attention of would-be donors, they need to be as compelling as possible, too.

By putting some thought into your letter and appeal package and paying attention to key details, you can increase both the number and size of gifts received from your mailings.

Here are nine ways to help give your 2009 appeal letters more of what it takes to move readers to make gifts:

1. Keep letters brief, neatly spaced, error free and grammatically correct.

2. Verify spelling of all names and proper titles of each individual.

3. Avoid use of words you wouldn't use in normal, everyday conversations. You don't want to look as if you studied your thesaurus just to impress them, and you don't want your readers to have to get out the dictionary to understand your message.

4. Use emotional adjectives sparingly. Almost every appeal leans heavily on "urgent" needs and "critical" situations. Convey your message with less-used but still-familiar, moving words.

5. Watch punctuation. Too many italicized, boldfaced or underlined passages clutter your page and detract from the message. Use exclamation marks only in proper context, not as an attention-getting gimmick.

6. Remember: Writing a short letter takes more effort than writing a long one. Ask an objective staff member to help with the editing process to make your piece as concise as possible while still having the impact you desire.

7. Don't send your first draft. Read your letter two or three times, or until all superfluous wording is eliminated.

8. Sign your name in real ink. Time taken to sign in a contrasting ink color shows you take a personal interest.

9. Be descriptive and direct. Writing "volunteers spent more than 100 hours each weekend collecting canned goods" tells your story much better than cliches such as: "We are striving to set new standards of excellence in the services we offer to those in need."

PROFITABLE DIRECT MAIL IDEAS

Generational Segmenting Boosts Response Rate

It was music to the ears of supporters of Manchester College (North Manchester, IN).

Staff at the liberal arts college took a clever approach to generational segmenting by using song titles and experienced a 3 percent increase in its response rate.

Janeen Kooi, director, The Manchester Fund, segmented more than 7,100 lybunt (gave last year but not this) and sybunt (gave some years but not this) alumni, parents and friends into five groups. Each group received a greeting card with a generationally appropriate song title, photo and corresponding tagline.

"Although all received the same message about the needs of the college, the tagline and the greeting message were segmented to match the song title," Kooi says.

"The song title was chosen to elicit an emotional response and to motivate action. For instance, research shows that 'civics' (those of the World War II era) respond to duty, responsibility and helping the next generation. So, the message was to 'Let the Good Times Roll,' as they did for you, for another generation of Manchester College students by making a gift to the college's annual fund."

In addition to "Let the Good Times Roll," Kooi carefully chose the following song titles: "Stand by Me" (alumni from the 1950s-'60s), "Imagine" (alumni from the 1970s) and "You are the Wind Beneath My Wings" (alumni from the 1980s, as well as parents and friends).

Once she determined the song title, Kooi wrote the tag lines and worked

An appeal for The Manchester Fund for Manchester College (North Manchester, IN) features greeting cards designed with specific constituent groups in mind. This is the card used for alumni from the 1950s and '60s.

with the college's archivist to find photos representing the corresponding time period. Parents and friends received a photo of recent and current students with a current professor.

While a complete data analysis is yet to occur, Kooi says the pictures, song titles and messages resonated with the donors.

Source: Janeen Kooi, Director of The Manchester Fund, Manchester College, North Manchester, IN.
Phone (260) 982-5202.
E-mail: jwkooi@manchester.edu.
Website: www.manchester.edu

Content not available in this edition

Boost Your Appeal's Response Rate With a Johnson Box

One way to get the key message of your solicitation letter heard is to use a Johnson Box.

A Johnson Box, placed at the very top of the letter above the salutation, is a centered, rectangular box containing the key message you want your reader to remember most. Pioneer direct mail copywriter Frank H. Johnson created the Johnson Box some 60 years ago.

Ivan Levison, Direct Response Copywriting (Greenbrae, CA), shares five tips for using a Johnson Box:

1. **Include the right content.** The box could contain a quote, the reason you're contacting them or an important announcement.

2. **Use it in the right letter.** If you're sending a non-personalized letter that's going out bulk rate in a window envelope using teaser copy, a Johnson Box will fit right in. But if you're writing a first-class letter in a closed-face envelope, the box will look out of place.

3. **Make it the right size.** If you're mailing an 8 1/2 X 11-inch letter, you want the box and the salutation line, to appear above the fold.

4. **Use an appropriate shape.**

5. **Include it in your next e-solicitation.** Run a line above and below the text rather than enclosing it in a box. The Johnson Box should fit easily into the reader's auto-preview box.

Source: Ivan Levison, Direct Response Copywriting, Greenbrae, CA. Phone (415) 461-0672.
E-mail: ivan@levison.com

PROFITABLE DIRECT MAIL IDEAS

Creative Solicitation Draws Donors

Philabundance, a food rescue organization in Philadelphia, has seen an increase in gifts from renewals and acquisitions by using a brown bag appeal that draws attention to both the mailing and the organization's mission.

The sealed brown paper lunch bag serves as the envelope, not for the appeal letter, but for the reply card and return envelope. The appeal letter is printed right on the back of the bag.

"The appeal not only gets noticed when someone opens their mailbox, it gets across the fact that the organization is trying to feed people," says Eleanor Missimer, director of annual giving.

The organization's brown bag appeal is sent for the fall renewal and acquisition, says Missimer.

"We see an 8 to 10.5 percent return on renewals, and a 1.3 to 1.5 percent return on acquisitions," she says. The average gift for renewals is $45 to $55, while the average gift for acquisitions is $30 to $35.

Source: Eleanor Missimer, Director of Annual Giving, Philabundance, Philadelphia, PA.
Phone (215) 339-0900, ext. 269.

Content not available in this edition

Analyze Appeal To Improve Future Results

Which of your direct mail appeals was most productive last year? Which resulted in the greatest dollar return? What was the average gift size from each mailing? How much did it cost to raise each dollar?

It makes good sense to monitor and analyze your direct mail costs and results throughout the course of each year and prior to drafting an operational plan for the upcoming year. Doing so will provide a quantitative measure of what works and what doesn't work.

Complete a direct mail cost analysis report (example shown at right) to track costs and results of solicitation appeals throughout the year.

Content not available in this edition

PROFITABLE DIRECT MAIL IDEAS

Learn to Write Effective Fundraising Letters

What makes an effective appeal letter? Should it be brief or lengthy? Formal or informal?

Although there are certain principles you can follow in creating a results-oriented letter, there is a great deal of flexibility in the shape such a letter can take. For instance, someone who is familiar with and supportive of your organization will generally be willing to read a longer letter, while it's best to send a one-page (or less) letter to someone less familiar with your cause.

Follow these guidelines to improve the effectiveness of your written appeals:

1. Have a strong sense of what your letter is going to say before you begin writing. What key message do you want to convey? What will be the make-up of those receiving the letter — past donors, nondonors, persons with some connection to your organization and its services, businesses?

2. Although you may be directing your letter to a large number of would-be contributors, the message should appear personal and informal — just one person speaking to another.

3. Be specific about what kind of response you expect.

4. Your letter should ask for only one thing, but the letter should also provide all the information your reader needs to comply with your request.

5. If you're unable to personalize your salutation to each recipient, rather than using a generic address such as "Dear Friends," consider an attention-grabbing headline or a question that calls for a yes answer. That first line should summon up good feelings and set the tone for the body of the letter to come.

6. In the body of your letter, use simple words that speed communication. Use active, concrete and colorful words. Use simple, direct sentences.

7. It's acceptable to underline or capitalize key words or phrases, but don't overdo it. Also consider handwritten inserts or marginal notes and subheads within the body of long letters. These devices help to move the reader in your intended direction.

8. The closing, and signature and title can lend authority to your message if the name is familiar or the person's title is prestigious.

9. The postscript can be the most effective part of the letter. You can use it to repeat the theme, reinforce your response deadline or suggest a further step, such as urging donors to increase their giving to certain levels.

Timeline Helps Visualize Your Direct Mail Flow

How detailed is your direct mail production schedule for the fiscal year?

The use of a direct mail production schedule helps everyone in the advancement department see the big picture and anticipate what needs to be done when — and by whom — to keep all mailings on track. The production cycle of each direct mail piece — from writing to drop dates — can be more easily anticipated to ensure deadlines are being met. Such a schedule also helps planners visualize when various groups will receive direct mail to better plan broad-based cultivation procedures and anticipate the flow of incoming gift revenue.

If you're not already doing so, develop a direct mail production schedule similar to the example at right to aid you in planning and visualizing your mailings for the entire year.

Content not available in this edition

Fundraising for Beginners: Essential Procedures for Getting a Fundraising Program Up and Running

CONNECTING WITH DONORS AND WOULD-BE DONORS BY PHONE

Gone are the days when a handful of phone numbers and a telephone add up to fundraising success. Today's telesolicitation efforts are far more advanced and require training callers (both paid and volunteer) who focus on making targeted calls with high-impact messages. The time you put into planning a phonathon will help ensure its success.

Anatomy of a Successful Phonathon

What components make up a successful phonathon?

Amber Asbjornsen, assistant director of annual giving, Western Washington University Foundation (Bellingham, WA), shares what makes her phonathon a success: "We set goals, make callers aware of their goals and monitor progress using statistics, caller feedback and prospects' comments. We use nightly incentives from local businesses to motivate callers and offer quarterly raises based on money raised and the ability to meet goals in categories (e.g., pledge percentage, average gift, matching gifts, credit card gifts, etc.). We create a team environment that callers love being a part of and have quarterly parties to celebrate successes. Positive feedback is a huge motivating factor and we do as much of it as we can (e.g., awarding a caller of the week, sending daily e-mails to congratulate callers on a good night, sending a weekly newsletter to keep callers informed and list top callers for specific categories, etc.)."

Last year, the foundation's phonathon raised $545,630, which was 18 percent of their overall annual fund revenue. Forty-five to 50 students were paid to call Sunday through Thursday from October to June, excluding holidays, finals and school breaks, says Asbjornsen. Callers made nearly 40,000 contacts last year. "We call prospects who have given between $1 and $999 or who have never given through the phonathon," says Asbjornsen. "Anyone who makes higher-level gifts is solicited through

the President's Club Campaign or for a major gift. Occasionally, we'll call President's Club prospects if they haven't responded to other solicitations."

Callers call from one large room with no cubicles, says Asbjornsen. "It's important to interact and socialize with one another. The job can be tough but having a neighbor to talk to helps build a stronger team dynamic. It also helps to seat new callers next to more experienced callers so they can hear what works and how experienced callers use rebuttals, make conversation, etc."

Source: Amber Asbjornsen, Assistant Director of Annual Giving, Western Washington University Foundation, Bellingham, WA. Phone (360) 650-3027. E-mail: amber.asbjornsen@wwu.edu

If Your Telesolicitation Includes Volunteer Callers

Special considerations should be taken if you're working with an all-volunteer bank of callers. These include:

1. Recruiting 30 percent more volunteers for your phonathon than are needed, anticipating not everyone will show up as expected.

2. Spacing veteran callers next to rookies to help when and if needed. Close proximity also allows new callers to hear how to make contacts with confidence and ease.

3. Whenever a caller receives a pledge for a minimum amount, say $100 or more, adding excitement to the calling by rewarding the caller with an inexpensive prize and having his/her name placed in a drawing for a more significant (but donated) prize.

How to Prepare Callers

Preparing callers starts as early as the interview process, says Asbjornsen.

"We conduct group interviews with the goal that by the end of the 90 minutes they will have a great understanding of what the phonathon is about as they answer questions about the importance of giving back, the impact of donations on campus and how comfortable they would be asking for money," she says.

Interviewees also conduct a mock call during the interview. Following the interview, hired callers go through six more hours of training, including time with call software. Their first few calls are made to an experienced caller for practice. During their first shift, they are paired with a caller mentor. They listen to the caller mentor for about an hour before making their first live calls. Returning callers receive advanced caller training annually.

"Quarterly caller evaluations help callers understand how important each element of the call is, how they can improve and how they stand according to our goals," says Asbjornsen. "We also have a call monitor who listens in on calls to provide caller feedback."

CONNECTING WITH DONORS AND WOULD-BE DONORS BY PHONE

Change in Script Wording Increases Phonathon Gifts

Taking the time to fine-tune your phonathon script should pay off in added gifts.

For the annual phonathon for US Lacrosse (Baltimore, MD) — the national governing body of lacrosse — Valerie Lambert, associate director of financial development, incorporated two changes into the organization's calling script that she says resulted in their callers having a great deal more success.

"Instead of asking, 'Would you be able to contribute?,' callers asked, 'HOW MUCH would you be able to contribute?'" says Lambert. "And once someone was willing to donate, rather than asking, 'Would you like to put this on a credit card?,' callers asked, 'WHICH credit card would you like to put this on?'"

The first year they incorporated these changes, says Lambert, 12 percent of donations were put on credit cards. The second year, she says, 20 percent of donations were put on credit cards. The average gift increased each year as well.

"I saw the greatest success with the college student callers who paid attention during the orientation and followed the script," she says. "We had one evening with 48 percent of the gifts put on credit cards. This means cash in hand the very next day."

Source: Valerie Lambert, Associate Director of Financial Development, US Lacrosse, Baltimore, MD. Phone (410) 235-6882, ext. 127. E-mail: vlambert@uslacrosse.org

Other Changes Lead to Additional Phonathon Success

Valerie Lambert, associate director of financial development, US Lacrosse (Baltimore, MD), shares additional strategies she has implemented for the phonathon program that have resulted in an increase in gifts:

✓ **Personalizing the script** — Incorporated a personalized, mail-merged script onto every donor sheet. (Previously, callers had a script on one sheet of paper and donor card on another sheet).

✓ **Keeping time zones in mind** — Sorted state folders by time zone, adding this field to data and call sheet. Each caller's information packet included a map of the country with time zones noted so when callers came back to a sheet later in the evening, they knew local time for the constituent simply by looking at the sheet and their time zone map.

✓ **Determining ask amount for each donor** — Personalized ask amounts according to the largest amount given, rather than all donor forms having the same suggested amounts.

✓ **Asking donors to increase gifts** — Incorporated into the script the largest giving amount and an ask that reflected a 50-percent increase.

✓ **Doublechecking contact info** — For verification purposes, printed on all call sheets all known contact information (address, phone numbers, and e-mails) as well as spouse name. The back of the sheet had a designated area for updating contact information.

✓ **Adding documentation** — Included an area on the back of the buckslip for tribute gift information, matching gift information, etc.

✓ **Adding tracking mechanisms, too** — Coded both the buckslip and enclosed return envelope as Phonathon 20XX so that the appeal could be easily tracked.

✓ **Spotlighting online giving** — Encouraged donors with a text box near the stamp area on the return envelope to "save time and money" by going to an area on the organization's website (www.uslacrosse. org/contribute) to make a gift. This hyperlink directly correlated to a phonathon appeal code.

Holding a Phonathon on a Shoestring Budget

If your organization is just getting a fundraising program under way, you don't have to be all that sophisticated to initiate your first phonathon. In fact, you can get any associated costs covered with cash and in-kind donations.

To telephone everyone on your mailing list for a first-time contribution, follow these simple steps:

1. Find a business with multiple phone lines that is willing to donate use of its bank of phones for a week during evening hours and over a portion of the weekend. Make sure the contribution includes the business' willingness to pay for long-distance phone calls as well.

2. Find a donor or donors to underwrite the cost of printed supplies and postage associated with the phonathon — pledge cards, envelopes, return envelopes, etc.

3. Enlist sufficient numbers of volunteers to fill the designated calling times throughout the phonathon. Example: Nine phones over five nights and one Sunday afternoon may require about 50 volunteers, assuming no one works more than one time.

4. Get a handful of businesses to provide incentive gifts/prizes to award productive volunteer callers and teams (e.g., anyone who lands a pledge for $100 or more; anyone who secures 10 or more pledges).

Don't let the fact that you've never done a phonathon before dissuade you. The important thing: Just do it.

CONNECTING WITH DONORS AND WOULD-BE DONORS BY PHONE

Telesolicitation Can Increase Donor Participation Rate

Looking for ways to increase the donor participation rate among your constituency? Telemarketing strategies can certainly help boost your numbers.

Here's how to increase your donor participation rate by phone:

- Secure a challenge gift and inform nondonors that all new gifts to the annual effort will be matched dollar for dollar.

- Send a postcard menu of (affordable) gift opportunities two weeks prior to your phoning blitz.

- Divide your nondonor population into specific groups and target them by phone to support specific projects.

- Offer a special gift or incentive to those who make first-time gifts — calendar, cookbook, etc.

- Make an effort to match callers to nondonors they know.

- Compare your nonprofit's existing participation rate with similar organizations that have higher rates — establish a competitive spirit to surpass them.

- Rather than letting those called get by with "maybe," ask them to commit to a specific amount.

- Explain that your organization's chances for receiving foundation support will improve if you can demonstrate that a high percentage of your constituency contributes to your efforts financially.

- Ask nondonors for a gift in honor or in memory of someone they know and respect — former professor, retired agency employee or volunteer.

- Conduct a constituency survey among nondonors and ask them for a gift during the same call.

How to Divvy Up Phonathon Names

If you conduct annual or ongoing telesolicitation efforts in-house — using either volunteers or paid callers — how do you divide and distribute names of prospects among your callers? More importantly, why does it even matter how you distribute the names?

Here are some answers:

1. Give names of your most generous past contributors to veteran callers with a track record of success and who will give these donors the special attention they deserve.

2. Start new callers off with some thank-you calls to past contributors. This will help them start off with a positive frame of mind and build their confidence.

3. Include calls for both past contributors and non-contributors when distributing prospect cards.

If callers are going to be contacting nondonors for first-time gifts, it's important that they also experience some sure bets to keep them enthused.

4. Allow callers the opportunity to request names of certain persons with whom they are familiar if they believe doing so will increase the odds of a first-time or increased gift. Do not, however, allow callers to sort through the entire list on their own.

5. Have a method to your distribution of prospect cards based on your entire prospect pool. For instance, if your pool is very large and you might not get through the entire list, distribute calls to ensure you will attempt to reach all previous contributors.

Phonathon Calls: Turn 'Maybe' into 'Yes'

To help your phonathon callers convert "maybe" into "yes:"

1. Offer an incentive to donors who make a firm pledge (e.g., free tickets, inclusion in a drawing).

2. Secure a challenge gift that only recognizes pledges.

3. Consider a system in which callers offer to call back a day or two later, after the prospect has had time to think about a pledge.

4. Instruct the caller to hand the phone off to a "higher up" standing by and prepared to take those "maybe" calls.

Coach Callers on Overcoming Objections

When preparing for a phonathon or ongoing telesolicitation effort, be sure to include training on overcoming donor objections. Conduct some practice sessions and distribute an objections sheet that illustrates possible responses to particular objections.

Some of the donor objections you will want to address include:

- I'm unemployed at the moment
- I'm upset about [name of organization]
- I already gave
- I give to other charities
- My spouse makes those decisions
- Business is down
- I'm paying for my child's tuition
- I only hear from you when you want money
- Just take me off your list
- I can't afford to give enough

CONNECTING WITH DONORS AND WOULD-BE DONORS BY PHONE

Motivate Callers With Goals

Whether you use paid callers or volunteers to raise funds, be sure they have goals in mind. Quantifiable goals make the work more meaningful and energizing and can also be used competitively among individual callers and/or caller teams.

Here are a few examples of goals for telesolicitors:

- Make a minimum of 100 attempted calls each evening.

- Secure 10 or more new gifts from previous nondonors.

- Get 25 or more pledges throughout the course of the calling period.

- Ask each donor for a 20 percent increase over last year's gift.

- Don't take a break until you receive one new commitment of $100 or more.

- Thank 100 percent of those with whom you visit.

Telemarketing Tips

1. Have rookie callers seated next to productive veterans. They can listen and learn.

2. Handle rejection by thanking the contact and asking for his/her opinion about a matter affecting your organization. This helps the conversation conclude on a positive note.

3. If you reach an answering machine, try one of these methods: mention a day and time you will call back; hold all answering machine calls until the weekend since most people tend to take calls then; or leave a message that you're sorry you missed them and mention you will send a follow-up letter.

4. In addition to an overall phonathon goal, establish daily or nightly goals for your callers. Keep posting how much has been raised so far next to the daily goal.

5. Groom callers for next year's phonathon efforts by sending them a summary of the results at the end of your fiscal year.

Caller Evaluation Sheets Provide Valuable Feedback

Officials with The University of Dayton's Office of Annual Giving send a caller evaluation sheet with each pledge confirmation made during their phonathon.

It's hard for persons receiving the confirmations to miss the evaluation sheets, since they're sent on bright yellow paper, says Deborah L. Schroeder, assistant director of Telefund. She notes that at least 25 percent are returned.

"We thought the evaluations would be a good tool to use in coaching our callers," Schroeder says. "We wanted them to be able to get feedback from the alumni, parents and friends that they talk with in addition to the feedback we give them. It is also a great customer service vehicle for our donors."

The best evaluations are posted on a "Caller Wall of Fame."

Schroeder says respondents offer meaningful feedback, which she uses to troubleshoot problems and reward callers. She finds the added comments that donors write the most useful: "Some comments are very complimentary, and it makes the student callers feel really good about what they're doing on a nightly basis. Sometimes donors will write, 'Deserves a raise; I would hire them to work for me, or 'It's because of them that I gave!' It's those comments that help the callers understand why we do what we do."

Source: Deborah L. Schroeder, Assistant Director of Telefund, Office of Annual Giving, The University of Dayton, Dayton, OH. E-mail: schroedl@notes.udayton.edu

Content not available in this edition

CONNECTING WITH DONORS AND WOULD-BE DONORS BY PHONE

Strive to Get Firm Pledges

Be sure your phonathon callers know how to respond when a would-be contributor hesitates to commit. Here are two comebacks for dealing with a hesitant donor:

> **Prospect**: "I'm not sure what to contribute. Let me discuss it with my spouse first."

> **Caller (Option No. 1)**: "I understand. Would it be possible for you to give an estimate of what you might give? That helps us predict the overall success of our phonathon effort."

> **Caller (Option No. 2)**: "I respect your desire to make a joint decision. Is there a time I could call back tomorrow after you've determined the appropriate amount?"

Test Cold Calling as a Way to Acquire New Donors

Whether you'd like to bring in year-end dollars to boost your 2009 bottom line or start 2010 ahead of the game, one tried-and-true technique to consider is the cold call.

Calling current and former donors through annual phonathons is one reliable way nonprofits can renew gifts from these proven supporters. So why not test a targeted cold-call phoning effort exclusively aimed at non-donors?

Whether you use paid callers or volunteers, one caller or a dozen, conduct the effort over a two-week period or use a longer-term approach, be sure to create a script aimed at generating first-time gifts from those who have never given before. To achieve success:

1. **Select three funding projects from which donors can choose** rather than asking for general support. People like knowing how their gifts will be used, and your success rate will increase by offering clear-cut funding projects.

2. **Start small.** Ask for a modest gift — $15 or $25 — just to get these new individuals on board. Many people refuse to give just because they feel their modest contributions won't be appreciated or make any noticeable difference.

3. **Make it easy to give.** Offer credit card payments, installment payments — limit the number of payments for smaller gifts — and one-time cash payments.

4. **Offer special incentives.** Consider offering two or three inexpensive premiums for giving: free admission to an event, one-year membership in one of your clubs at a reduced rate or a calendar with photos that relates to your organization and its mission.

Your goal should be simply to acquire new donors regardless of gift size. Once that's accomplished you can focus on building a habit of giving.

Use this generic script aimed at non-donors as a starting point to create one for your cause:

Attract More Phonathon Volunteers

Need more volunteer callers willing to step up to the plate? Get someone to donate something of value: a weekend at a resort, an iPhone, a free six-month leased vehicle. Every five completed calls gets the caller one raffle ticket for the prize.

Caller Training Tip

Don't just point your phonathon calling volunteers to the phone and tell them, "go to it." Spend some time teaching them about the impact that gifts will have on your nonprofit and those you serve.

Be specific. Share some examples. Name names. Give your mission a face.

Clearly identify to the callers how important donations are to your cause and you will empower them with that knowledge and embolden them to enthusiastically ask others to support your cause.

Sample Phonathon Script Used for Non-donors

Caller:

Mr. Hansen, this is Marci Wiggins calling on behalf of the Acme Gospel Mission. We're making a special effort this year to contact every citizen in our community to invite support for one of three special funding projects — and we're not asking for much.

Specifically, we would like you to consider a $15 or $25 gift to support one of these important projects:

1. New bedding for those who need shelter at our facility.
2. Meals for those we serve. A gift of $15 will cover meal costs for one needy person for one day.
3. Counseling services gifts to help get our visitors back on track.

Mr. Hansen, if you could find it in your heart to make a $15 or $25 gift for any one of these projects, you will receive two donated tickets for the Feb. 15 circus performance at Acme Auditorium. Which of these worthwhile projects would you like to fund today?

Fundraising for Beginners: Essential Procedures for Getting a Fundraising Program Up and Running.
Edited by Scott C. Stevenson.
© 2009 Stevenson, Inc. Published 2009 by Stevenson, Inc.

FACE-TO-FACE ASKS: CORNERSTONE OF FUNDRAISING SUCCESS

Face-to-face solicitation is by far the most effective way to raise needed funds. Many with little prior experience fear asking for support. It's called call reluctance. But once you view the act of soliciting gifts properly, the experience becomes energizing. The most successful fundraisers are passionate about the cause for which they are raising funds.

Planning Is Key to Solicitation Calls

Planning and preparation are key elements to a successful major gift solicitation. As the development officer, it's your job to see that those involved in a solicitation of a major gift are well versed on four key aspects:

1. **The project.** If it's a team solicitation call, at least one member should have a thorough understanding of the funding project and be able to address technical questions that might arise.

2. **The written proposal.** Everyone involved in the solicitation should have an understanding of the proposal's contents: the project description, its budget and the executive summary.

3. **The prospect.** What's the prospect's relationship to your organization? What topics should be avoided? What are his/her primary funding interests?

4. **Each participant's role in the solicitation.** Who will be doing the asking? Who will be prepared to describe the funding opportunity in detail?

Presentation Tools for Face-to-face Calls

What resources do you rely on to help tell your message in face-to-face solicitations?

Thomas Lockerby, vice president for development, Boston College (Chestnut Hill, MA), says the presentation tools they use most often are printed materials.

"We use shorter impact pieces — cultivation pieces about how a gift might make a difference, or stewardship pieces, such as a set of faculty writings or a report from students about the importance of a scholarship," Lockerby says.

They gauge the best timing for introducing these materials on a case by case basis with each donor. "I generally introduce written materials during an oral discussion, perhaps in the middle of a conversation with a donor," he says, "although it ultimately depends on the prospect's interests and the nature of the material."

As a general rule, Lockerby says, they don't use electronic tools in major donor presentations: "In very rare cases we might share a PowerPoint presentation if making a strategic impact statement... or an architectural drawing if it is a building discussion."

Source: Thomas B. Lockerby, Vice President for Development, Boston College, Chestnut Hill, MA.

Practice Makes Perfect: Don't Shy Away From Asking

When it comes to soliciting major gifts, remember this: It's better to ask and make mistakes than it is to wait forever in your quest to perfect the close.

Will you make mistakes? Of course. Even the most accomplished solicitors make mistakes. That's how we learn. But don't let those mistakes stop you from pursuing major gifts. Keep asking and learning from your previous asks.

In addition to writing up a trip or call report after each solicitation, take the time to make some personal notes. List what went right during the call. Then write down what went wrong. Be honest with yourself.

By evaluating each call, you will learn that it's not so much your style or even your knowledge that determines a potential gift. Rather, it's your determination to keep asking.

Asking for the Gift

After you have formally solicited a prospect for a specific amount, remain silent until the prospect has fully responded. Silence can prove to be a valuable tool when used judiciously.

How to Lead Up To the Close

What do you talk about just before popping the question? What can you say that will set the stage for that final ask?

Although your answers will vary somewhat depending on individual circumstances, it is safe to say that, if you've done all of your cultivation homework in prior meetings, your comments leading up to the ask should involve reiterating some key elements of what's been said before.

Some examples of what you might have said in leading up to the close include:

- I know that based on our previous discussions, you have indicated an interest in participating in this campaign at some level.

- In past visits you have expressed a particular interest in funding [name of project]....

- Before I invite you to make your commitment, let me say that, in my opinion, your gift will clearly set the pace for those who follow.

- [Name of charity] has set out to achieve some extraordinary accomplishments over the next several years. And if we are to do that, it will require extraordinary sacrifice of everyone associated with our institution.

FACE-TO-FACE ASKS: CORNERSTONE OF FUNDRAISING SUCCESS

Swim With Solicitation Pros Who Know How to Ask

New to the development profession? Or could your solicitation skills perhaps use a bit of refining?

To polish your solicitation skills and learn more about the art of asking, spend time with those who have a track record of success. Identify two or three seasoned professionals and:

1. **Get them to talk about their fundraising style.** How do they know what to say and when to say it? Do they have some standard lines from which to choose?

2. **Watch them in action.** If you work for the same nonprofit, ask to accompany them on some calls to observe them in action.

3. **Invite them to critique you.** Whether you do some role-playing or they accompany you on some calls to observe your style, ask for honest feedback on specific ways you can improve your approach.

Include an Executive Summary With All Proposals

Do you follow a standard outline when crafting major gift proposals? Whether you do or not, make a point to include an executive summary at the beginning of your written document. The reason for that is two-fold:

1. If written properly, a proposal summary will tempt the potential donor to read on. As you draft the summary, attempt to view it through the eyes of the would-be donor. In 200 words or less, what can you say that will captivate the reader? Obviously, the proposed name of the fund or building project will draw attention. The way you describe the impact of the donor's gift may also come into play. If the donor has an obvious interest in the growth of a proposed endowment fund or the annual interest from it, for instance, you may want to devote more wordage to the way the gift will be invested and how it relates to your overall endowment.

2. Summaries will also help to ensure readers see the document's big picture if they choose to read no further. Knowing that could happen, the summary should include the ask amount, what the realization of that gift would

accomplish and the benefits to the donor for making that gift a reality. Do not include the payout period for your request; that's an item that can be negotiated as the gift is finalized.

Avoid These Solicitation Blunders

The following list represents 10 major errors fundraisers should avoid when calling on prospects:

1. Not asking for gifts
2. Not asking for a large enough amount
3. Not sharing donor benefits
4. Not listening
5. Not asking questions
6. Not knowing enough about the prospect before solicitation
7. Not being flexible
8. Not cultivating the donor
9. Asking for the gift too soon
10. Not knowing enough facts about your organization

Content not available in this edition

FACE-TO-FACE ASKS: CORNERSTONE OF FUNDRAISING SUCCESS

Understand the Procedure of a Solicitation Call

You've had several opportunities to cultivate your prospect. It's now time to solicit and close the sale. But what to do? Jump immediately to the question? Make small talk? Dive into your presentation?

There are six basic skills important in soliciting a major gift:

1. **The opening.** In any person-to-person exchange, the opening conversation will play a role in determining the outcome. The opening should set the tone for your visit and provide for a positive outcome. It is critical that you involve the prospect in what you're saying. One of the best ways to do this is by talking about a subject of great interest to the prospect, namely, himself or herself. Don't talk to your prospect, but rather with him or her. Drawing him/her out gives you a better chance at bringing that person into a meaningful relationship with your organization.

2. **Questioning.** Once you have your prospect's attention with the opening, keep that attention and deepen the prospect's involvement. During the questioning period, make the prospect aware of your nonprofit's need before you demonstrate how the prospect can meet that need. Don't ask questions that force a "yes" or "no" response. Rather, ask challenging questions that help uncover your prospect's motivations and needs. This form of questioning can provide the raw material you're looking for to incorporate as feedback when you make your presentation.

3. **Listening.** This is a skill that is easy to do but difficult to master. A good listener is a participant who understands communication is both an active and a selective process. Listen with a purpose. Ask questions and give feedback to your prospect so he/she knows you are hearing what was said. Try to be empathetic in your listening. Put yourself in your prospect's position. By doing this, you will build respect and improve your odds of achieving the desired results.

4. **Presenting.** In making the case for your organization and its needs, keep the needs of your prospect in mind. How can his/her investment in your organization benefit the donor? Talk about the benefits and advantages of the prospect's gift rather than the organization's operations and problems.

   Remember earlier portions of your conversation with the prospect and incorporate appropriate comments back into your presentation to build your case. Example: "Katherine, you mentioned earlier how important it is to address the needs of the poor in our community. This project would do just that! Here's how...."

5. **Overcoming objections.** Although most people are very uncomfortable with objections raised by others, it's important to remember that an objection is not an attack, but rather a question. Knowing this should help you overcome your discomfort.

   With an objection, always show understanding of your prospect's position. Gain your prospect's respect by responding, "I can understand why you would have that concern," or "I see your point of view." The main point is to let the prospect know his/her objection is acceptable, that others feel the same way, and that the prospect's question has helped in finding a constructive solution to the problem. All objections are really questions and the prospect's investment in the project will help overcome those objections as his/her knowledge about your organization grows. This will help you to convert the objections into reasons for giving.

6. **Asking.** Asking is synonymous with closing. After you have dealt will all the prospect's questions and concerns, it is now time to ask for the gift. Most failure in face-to-face solicitation comes because we do not properly ask for the gift. It is important that we know how and when to ask.

Always ask for more money than is expected, but not more than the prospect can give. This gives you a stronger negotiating position and in most cases helps get the gift most needed and wanted. The prospect knows that this is no ordinary meeting. You are present to discuss serious concerns that interest both the prospect and your organization.

Soliciting Tips....

- Rather than getting a prospect to think about an amount of money to give, get him/her to think about a project that costs money.

- Before making a call, ask yourself three times why the prospect should make this gift. This warm-up exercise will help to put you in the right frame of mind during your meeting.

- Try to anticipate a prospect's objections by answering them in your presentation.

FACE-TO-FACE ASKS: CORNERSTONE OF FUNDRAISING SUCCESS

Plan Ahead: Solicitation Strategies Worksheet

Going to ask for a major gift? Plan ahead by using this two-person solicitation strategies worksheet.

"It provides structure for people, so one doesn't dominate the conversation and so the process is thought out," says Jim Lewis, partner, Lewis Kennedy Associates (Portland, OR). "While one is conducting the conversation, the other can observe body language and listen."

The worksheet helps you outline who will say what, what the possible questions or objections might be and who will ask for the gift. "It forces some planning by people, so they just don't go out and wing it — which can be a disaster because in the middle of the conversation you may find out that one person doesn't really know the mission of the organization or why they are there," says Lewis.

Also, other than to provide structure, Lewis says, "It's designed to remove as much as possible the fear of gift asking." Being prepared and knowing the plan of action can not only eliminate any apprehensions, but can help make the ask go smoother, which may result in the desired gift.

Source: Jim Lewis, Partner, Lewis Kennedy Associates, Portland, OR. Phone (503) 236-4850, ext. 202. E-mail: jim@lewiskennedy.com

Content not available in this edition

Procedure Is Important for First-time Calls

When you're making a first-time call on a new prospect, the time you take for planning up front will improve your odds of success.

First, gather background information on the person with whom you will be meeting by visiting with individuals who have a relationship to both your nonprofit and the prospect. It's a big help if you can work through a willing mutual friend or associate. That way, when you call to set the appointment, you can say "I'm calling at the request of (name of mutual contact)."

Use an introductory visit as a way to introduce the value of your organization and find ways to seek the prospect's advice as a way of building ownership in your agency or institution. It's all about relationship building.

Once you have an appointment set, confirm it with a letter as well.

FACE-TO-FACE ASKS: CORNERSTONE OF FUNDRAISING SUCCESS

Tailor Presentations to Individuals' Interests

Learning to tailor individual presentations to would-be donors' interests is a craft that requires thorough prospect research and sensitive listening skills. That's why knowing as much as possible about prospects' interests prior to the solicitation is so important.

Sometimes prospects' interests will have a direct link to funding projects while at other times the relationship will be more abstract.

Whether through cultivation visits prior to solicitation or other research efforts, garner information to help identify your prospects' interests and shape your solicitation. At right are some categories to help you learn more about prospects:

Interest Categories, Key Facts

Here are some interest categories and important information that may be helpful to know about your major gift prospects:

Personal Interests
- Importance placed on family
- Leisure-time activities
- What matters most in life
- Importance placed on education
- Financial philosophy
- Philanthropic interests
- Civic involvement/interests
- Future hopes and plans
- Close friends
- Pet peeves
- Personal heroes
- Religious preference/importance

Political Persuasion
- Conservative versus liberal
- Passive versus strong opinions
- Opinions on social issues

Business/Career
- Career progression
- Current responsibilities
- Accomplishments and setbacks
- Business connections
- Management style
- Community, statewide and/or national involvement

Ground Rules for the First-time Solicitor

If you have volunteers who are just getting started in raising funds, here are some answers to basic questions that will get them off on the right foot:

I feel sheepish about begging people for money. How do I get around that?

It's all in how you look at it. Your job isn't to beg for money. Rather, you're giving people an opportunity to support a very deserving cause. You really need to believe that this cause is worth supporting. If you do, it will be reflected in your enthusiasm, and it won't feel like you're asking at all.

If I've been assigned calls to make, can't I just send the information to the prospect or leave it with his/her secretary to review?

Absolutely not. Whenever you accept responsibility for soliciting gifts or memberships, it's important that you see the prospect face to face. Doing so will help maximize your fundraising success, show the prospect you take his/her support seriously and provide an opportunity to make the prospect more aware of the charity's programs and services.

So I just stop by sometime and ask if he/she wants to make a gift?

If you want to do the best job possible, you first set an appointment with the prospect, explaining that you want to meet with him/her on behalf of the organization you're representing. Go on to explain, "I'll only need a few minutes of your time, however, it's important that I have an opportunity to meet with you face to face."

OK. So you've got me in the door. Now what?

That depends on the objective of your call. Have you been instructed to simply introduce the organization you represent? Is your goal to make the prospect feel more inclined to make a gift (cultivation)? Or do you intend to make your solicitation pitch? If the latter is true, there is a pattern your presentation can follow that goes from opening to questioning to listening to presenting to overcoming any objections and finally, asking for the gift.

It's best if you practice going through a presentation on your own a time or two in addition to making some calls with a veteran solicitor so you can observe as well as help support the presentation.

Can you offer any tips on asking?

Asking — or closing — comes at the end of your presentation, after you have dealt with all the prospect's questions and concerns. Begin by asking for a specific amount, generally more than is expected but not more than the prospect can give.

Then, once you've asked, difficult as it may be to do, remain silent. Wait for a response.

Finally, whether you walk away with a gift, a signed pledge or nothing, make a point to thank the prospect for having given you his/her time and attention.

Calculating the Ask

■ To determine how much to ask of an individual who has given consistently over time, multiply his/her average annual gift size times four. Then multiply that amount by five to estimate the total gift that could be made over a five-year period.

FACE-TO-FACE ASKS: CORNERSTONE OF FUNDRAISING SUCCESS

Sound Advice for Closing More Gifts

1. It's not how much you talk, it's how much your prospect speaks that will eventually mean the difference between a gift and no gift.

2. Make use of trial closes. Ask questions that measure the prospect's degree of commitment before your final ask: "Do you agree that this funding project is worthy of major support?"

3. Develop an arsenal of asks. It's helpful to have several different techniques from which to choose, depending on the circumstances.

4. Avoid questions that result in a "no" response. Instead, ask a question such as: "Would it be easier to contribute $1,000 if it were divided into monthly payments?"

5. Rely on the summary close as a common technique: The solicitor simply reminds the prospect of the intended use and benefits — for both the charity and the donor.

The strength of this close is in listing the benefits most important to the prospect immediately before asking for action.

Make a Habit Of Face-to-face Calls

If making calls on prospects is a high priority, establish a routine to see that it happens without question. Here's one procedure for doing so:

Once each week, write down the names of five or more people you need to contact the following week. Rank these names in order of importance and list the objective of your visit (e.g., introduction, cultivation, solicitation, stewardship). Then contact each individual to set an appointment for the following week.

This weekly habit helps ensure you follow through on this critical part of your job.

Don't Let Your Presentation Go Flat

If your job responsibilities include making regular calls on individuals and/or businesses — and you've been doing so for some time — be careful that you don't start sounding like a broken record. When you use the same presentation day in and day out, it's easy for your pitch to become stale.

It may be time to remind yourself to become more enthusiastic in your delivery. Listen to what you are saying. What should it mean to the prospect? Are there portions of your presentation that should be changed or dropped?

To avoid sounding flat, develop more than one presentation format. Test new phrases and sales approaches. Experiment to find out what works and what doesn't.

Keep in mind that by trying new approaches, you'll find it more necessary to pay attention to what's being said. You'll also find it easier to show enthusiasm. And more enthusiasm will undoubtedly boost your success.

Make Use of a Monthly Calls Planner

Whether you track your prospect calls productivity by inputting information into a computer program, penciling it into a pocket calendar or something in between, know that planning calls over a 30-day period will help you to improve that productivity.

A monthly calls planner helps to:

1. Ensure you are designating sufficient time to face-to-face calls.

2. Aid in making the best use of available time.

3. Serve as a valuable accountability tool for you (and/or your supervisor).

4. Prioritize who most merits a personal call.

5. Meet monthly call objectives (e.g., 25 calls per month).

6. Monitor the types of calls that are being made (e.g., solicitation, cultivation, etc.).

Use this monthly calls planner template to create your own.

MONTHLY CALLS PLANNER

Name _____   Month _____

Appointment Considerations & Confirmed Appointments

| Date | Donor/Prospect | Phone | Appointments | | Purpose/Comments |
			Time	Location	
1	Tony Perhlman	454-4334	9:30	His office	Follow-up solicitation
	Ray/Marti Tu	446-7890	11:45	Minerva's	Solicitation
2	Lipper, Inc.	276-7737	8:30	Office	Introduction, inquiry
	Alice Stoneking	576-8382	2:00	Her home	Cultivation call
3	Marshall King	447-5321	Noon	Bill's Diner	Stewardship: Scholarship info
4					
5	Mary Persing	266-9022	9:00	Her office	Solicitation
	Stone Data	232-4420	11:00	Her office	Solicitation: sponsorship

SPECIAL EVENTS GARNER ANNUAL GIVING SUPPORT

Although some nonprofits with a long history of fundraising tend to shy away from special events and consider them labor intensive, there's no doubt that special events have multiple benefits. In addition to raising need funds, they attract new contributors, they raise awareness, they offer another avenue of giving for those who might not otherwise contribute and more. Special events come in all forms and sizes and provide a great opportunity for volunteer involvement in your fund development efforts.

Consider Sharing a Special Events Manager

Can't justify the cost of hiring a full-time special events director? Why not partner with two or three dissimilar nonprofits and jointly hire a special events manager who can organize special events on behalf of each organization throughout the year?

Perhaps each nonprofit would get the professional's full attention during particular months and the special events and dates would be agreed on in advance.

The participating nonprofits would obviously need to discuss and agree on key issues prior to hiring the events professional. And those organizations would bear some responsibility for supporting and assisting the professional in various ways, such as supplying the volunteers needed for an event.

If you want the benefits realized from special events but can't justify the position, consider this partnership arrangement.

Create a Comprehensive Sponsorship Menu

Most event planners prepare sponsorship proposals for a particular event. Why not create a menu that lists *all* sponsorship opportunities that exist throughout the year — one that includes every sponsorship opportunity available for all your events and programs?

A comprehensive sponsorship opportunities menu can be used when meeting with would-be sponsors for the first time. This comprehensive wish list of sponsorships allows would-be sponsors to identify and select those that most appeal to them — a key advantage.

At right is a simple example of such a menu you can use as a guide in creating a document that works best for you. The menu could be incorporated into a proposal or prepared as a stand-alone handout. It could also be distributed via direct mail and include a bounce back which allows the recipient to request additional information.

A sample comprehensive sponsorship menu that can be used by your organization to present every sponsorship opportunity available for all events and programs.

Special Event Follow-up

Special events help to broaden your base of support. They create relationships where none may have previously existed. That's why it's important to take crucial follow-up steps after a completed fundraising event.

Send personal thank-you letters to everyone who attended and may have also given in other ways: purchased auction items, served as sponsors, purchased a raffle ticket and more. Acknowledge those acts in your letter of thanks.

Don't allow a special event to turn into a one-time connection. Use that opportunity to forge relationships with all attendees.

MARENGO PUBLIC SCHOOL
2008-09 Sponsorship Opportunities

Marengo Golf/Tennis Classic
Overall sponsor.............................$10,000
Golf sponsor $5,000
Tennis sponsor $2,500
Golf clinic...$750
Tennis clinic.....................................$250
Social hour......................................$500
Dinner/program $500
Holes/tees (18).......................$120 each

Theatre: Fall performance
Overall sponsor............................$2,500
Program sponsor...........................$500
Post-performance reception $500

Sponsor a debater
Limit of 20................................$200 each
The sponsors of this year's debate program will help underwrite travel, lodging and meals associated with our student debate team.
You will also be special guests at our Debate Invitational and meet our debaters at a special reception following the event.

> *For more info: Contact Betsy Swan, 282-0553*

Annual lecture series
5 lectures .... $3,000 each
We will host five lectures throughout the year. This year's theme is "values worth protecting." The events are geared to students but open to the public.

Marengo career day
Event sponsor................................$1,000
Career panel (5)......................$250 each
Luncheon sponsor $500

Marengo holiday performance
Overall sponsor.............................$2,000
Holiday reception $500
Regional tour sponsors.......$3,000 each

Marengo Band:
Fall, spring performances
Fall sponsor $1,000
Spring sponsor $1,000

Faculty fall retreat...................$5,000
Each August, Marengo faculty are invited to participate in a three-day professional development and planning session. Outside speakers and facilitators are enlisted for a productive and motivational experience.

For information about athletic sponsorship opportunities, contact Alex Martin: 282-0564

SPECIAL EVENTS GARNER ANNUAL GIVING SUPPORT

Generating New Life for an Old Event

Fundraising events that have been around for decades can be prestigious, must-attend affairs that generate amazing revenue off their name alone. Or, they can start to lose steam — and money. When the latter happens, it's time to assess the event itself and, if you decide to stick with it, find fresh ideas to generate fresh attendees and funds.

For instance, when the Phoenix (AZ) Zoo's 18-year-old ZooFari event was in a slump, zoo officials gave it a much-needed boost by:

1. Changing the event's details;

2. Marketing the event to a new audience; and

3. Switching committee members every year.

Kelly Balthazor, the zoo's corporate development manager, says for years the ZooFari event boasted tastings from Phoenix's best chefs. But as other nonprofits caught on to this style of event, they saw attendance at the zoo event fall.

So in 2000, Balthazor and her staff revamped the event. They kept the popular chef tastings but incorporated new things, like a new layout every year, different entertainment and new revenue streams to keep guests having fun.

She also marketed the event to new audiences. Since many of the original attendees had stopped coming, she worked with media partners to find new audiences. After three years, the buzz got back around that the ZooFari event was the event to attend.

Another important part of keeping the event fresh was revamping the committee members every year. She admits that doing so can be a challenge because of the possibility of hurting long-standing members' feelings, but that it helps to point out the extra revenue the changes are bringing and what's best for the zoo.

She says the challenges of turning the event around are staff time needed to do so. But, she says, it's worth it: The event that brought in $185,000 in 2000 was able to increase revenue to $288,000.

Source: Kelly Balthazor, Corporate Development Manager, The Phoenix Zoo, Phoenix, AZ. Phone (602) 914-4309. E-mail: kbalthazor@thephxzoo.com

Insider Tips for Planning Your Event

1. To help pre-sell tickets and recognize past attendees, give the previous year's participants a chance to buy tickets before a specified date.

2. Make planning your special event a special experience for your committee. Incorporate portions of your event (e.g., a CD of the musical performers, samples of special desserts or appetizers) into the planning process.

3. Develop strategies to sell 75 percent of the event's tickets prior to sending invitations.

4. Select an event that appeals to your constituency and is consistent with their pocketbooks.

Events That Attract Persons of Wealth

Organize it and they will come. If you want to attract persons of means to your nonprofit, focus on events that capture their attention, keeping your organization's mission in mind.

Here are events to attract financially secure individuals:

- Wine tasting fundraiser
- Investment celebrity speaker
- Art exhibition reception
- Gourmet foods fundraiser with notable chefs
- Seminars on exotic travel
- Fashion show fundraiser
- Reception for visiting dignitaries
- String quartet performance and reception
- Fundraiser open to Harley Davidson motorcycle owners
- Estate planning seminar

Special Events Help Build Your Database

Unless you represent an organization such as a college or university that has a ready-made constituency of would-be donors (graduates), it's important to implement strategies to help build a list of interested individuals and businesses.

While not all special events raise huge amounts of money, they do help increase awareness and attract those who may become repetitive contributors. Special events also serve as a way for volunteers to become involved with your organization and its work. And as you know, involvement leads to investment.

To attract involvement and build your database, plan a yearlong special events schedule that will reach out to individuals and businesses in your community. If you're just getting started, limit your events to two or three, but make them different enough (e.g., golf classic, gala, celebrity waiter luncheon) to appeal to varied community segments.

Get volunteers involved from the start to encourage their full ownership of each event's success.

SPECIAL EVENTS GARNER ANNUAL GIVING SUPPORT

Theme Park Is Site for Hospital's Birthday Party

At a Glance —	
Event Type:	Birthday party/ community fundraiser
Gross:	$160,000
Costs:	$70,000
Net Income:	$90,000
Volunteers:	200
Planning:	9-12 months
Attendees:	4,500
Revenue Sources:	Sponsorships, ticket sales, raffles, children's activities
Unique Feature:	Held at a local theme park

Every special event has its perfect location: For a Western-theme event, nothing beats a hay bale-filled barn. For a murder mystery event, a dimly lit mansion is ideal. And a sports-themed event is a natural for a local sports stadium.

How about a birthday party that could conceivably be attended by thousands?

An amusement park more than fills the bill as the perfect venue for "Magee's Birthday Party," an annual community fundraiser for Magee-Womens Hospital of UPMC (Pittsburgh, PA).

The event celebrating the more than 525,000 babies born at the hospital in its 98-year history is held at Kennywood, a Pittsburgh-area theme park.

Beyond celebrating people born at the hospital, the event introduces new services and raises funds for Magee programs.

The hospital's foundation executive director approached Kennywood officials with the idea for the birthday party in 2002 after he wanted to host a large community event where all Magee families could celebrate together, says Denise Wickline, event coordinator.

Since then, they have secured Kennywood for a day and

negotiated other opportunities for use of its facilities, including help advertising in the park during the year and opening more rides and concessions when attendance increases.

The event, which attracts 4,500 guests annually, involves a day of rides within the park, raffle, entertainment, local personalities and children's activities.

At the 2008 event, raffle ticket sales generated $7,000, with an additional $2,000 raised from the sale of the grand prize tickets.

With ticket sales ($20 each or five for $75), sponsorship revenue ($103,000), raffle sales ($9,000) and Kiddieland activity sales ($700), says Wickline, the event saw a net income of $90,000.

Source: Denise Wickline, Event Coordinator, Magee-Womens Foundation, Pittsburgh, PA. Phone (412) 641-8911. E-mail: dwickline@magee.edu

Content not available in this edition

Content not available in this edition

SPECIAL EVENTS GARNER ANNUAL GIVING SUPPORT

Give Donors Easy Access to Where Their Money Goes

Want a surefire way to make sure event guests, donors and sponsors return year after year? Make sure they know specifically where their money is going and give them easy access to that information.

If the event is a large one for your organization, you most likely already have a section of your website devoted to it. You also probably steer inquiries about the event to that location. So why not add a tab, link or page entitled "Where Your Money Goes," and then tell them?

The Conservation Gala, which supports programs of the Credit Valley Conservation Foundation (Mississauga, Ontario, Canada) and the Conservation Halton Foundation (Milton, Ontario, Canada), has its own website (www.conservationgala.ca).

The website details where the funds raised at the last two Conservation Gala events have gone.

Specifically, the website states that the funds have gone to:

- "Support the 2006 Halton Children's Water Festival at Kelso Conservation Area in Milton.

Thanks to your support and a volunteer crew of 600 enthusiastic teachers and high school students, more than 3,000 children attended the festival."

- "Support several environmental projects including the Rattray Marsh Living Discovery Centre, a contemporary and unique living Discovery Centre at Rattray Marsh Conservation Area; Black Creek Restoration Project, a tree planting and restoration project along Black Creek south of Georgetown."

The numbers and project details offer a concrete picture of where the funds are going in terms that most people will understand while also indicating a high level of accountability and stewardship of donor funds, which Hardwar says adds up to an event and an organization donors want to support.

Source: Sharlene Hardwar, Partnership Development Coordinator, Credit Valley Conservation Foundation, Mississauga, Ontario, Canada. Phone (905) 670-1615. E-mail: shardwar@creditvalleycons.com. Website: www.conservationgala.ca

Sponsorships Help Alleviate Expenses

With 44 sponsors at three giving levels — plus numerous in-kind donations — organizers of the Chefs' Feast 2008 are able to use nearly all the money raised to support childhood feeding programs of Lowcountry Food Bank (Charleston, SC).

Chefs' Feast 2008, in its ninth year, raised $195,200, with less than 5 percent of its gross revenue ($4,800) going to expenses.

"Whether it's the chefs, printing, design or lighting, everything is donated," says Miriam Coombes, development and communications coordinator.

Sponsors' past generosity helps them to continue to fund the event, she says. "When we show new sponsors how previous sponsors have supported this event, they're impressed with how much others have come to the table for our cause."

Sponsorship levels include: Signature, $25,000; Event, $5,000; and Corporate, $2,500. More than $100,000 was generated in sponsor tables.

Guests enjoy food prepared by 23 chefs from the organization's 10-county region; the chefs are personally invited by Chef Robert Carter of Peninsula Grill to participate.

Source: Miriam Coombes, Development and Communications Coordinator, Lowcountry Food Bank, Charleston, SC. Phone (843) 747-8146. E-mail: mcoombes@ lcfbank.org

Quick Tip to Snatch a Sponsor

To snare potential sponsors, consider what aspects of your event would appeal to them.

Will they be most excited about the event itself? Emphasize the social, political, environmental or economic facets that may intrigue a sponsor.

Will the unique venue or entertainment connect the sponsor to your event? Or is your cause or mission enough of a draw?

Publicity, if you can promise and deliver it, is highly enticing to many sponsors.

Don't approach all potential

sponsors with the same general appeal. Tailor your pitch to specific interests. Bring attention to smaller aspects, such as staging or decorations, and give sponsors a chance to fund and attach their names to these aspects.

Source: Gravely Wilson, Associate Director of Development Events, Denver Art Museum, Denver, CO. Phone (720) 865-5000.

At a Glance —

Event Type:	Chefs' Feast
Gross:	$200,000
Costs:	$4,800
Net Income:	$195,200
Volunteers:	125
Attendees:	900 to 950
Revenue Sources:	Sponsorships, ticket sales
Unique Feature:	Eclectic mixture of guests, food

SPECIAL EVENTS GARNER ANNUAL GIVING SUPPORT

Creative Ways to Attract New Donors to Your Fundraiser

Keeping your event fresh and attractive to new donors can be quite a challenge.

So what can your organization do to bring fresh faces and pocketbooks to your next fundraising event, while keeping your loyal supporters wanting to come back for more year after year?

Kathy Steil, program coordinator, Cheyenne Regional Medical Center Foundation (Cheyenne, WY), knows a thing or two about attracting new donors. For 20 years, the Cheyenne Regional Medical Center Foundation has held its annual Denim 'N' Diamonds campaign — with growing success.

What began in 1990 with 150 guests attending a fashion show, dinner/dance and silent auction netting more than $75,000 has evolved into an event seating 940 guests netting more than $300,000.

Steil shares some tried-and-true formulas she uses for the annual fundraiser that other organizations can use to keep attendance on the rise:

- **Select a one-of-a-kind venue.** Pique guests' curiosity by holding the event at a "not your run-of-the-mill" venue (e.g., ice rink/hockey center, ranch, football field, etc.).

- **Keep the theme changing.** While the foundation's campaign is always called Denim 'N' Diamonds, its theme is always changing. Past themes include an Asian-inspired event and a Wild West theme.

- **Create outstanding, unforgettable invitations.** Capture your guests' attention as soon as they open the mailbox. Start with the envelope and carry the theme through to the invitations and RSVP cards. "Incredible artwork for the invitations can set the stage for a whole event," says Steil. Past invitations have come in all sizes and have been packaged in boxes and folders. While invitations have been mailed, sometimes all 1,200 have been hand-delivered by volunteers.

- **Host a pre-event party.** Entice new donors to your event by hosting a major sponsor cocktail supper or other before-the-event event in a unique venue or home that has sparked the community's interest. "The key to this event," says Steil, "is to have it hosted by a specific donor or small group of donors who are willing to spend $6,000 to $10,000 for a great party and to hold it in a place everyone wants to see but hasn't yet."

- **Select well-respected, well-known honorary chairs.** Selecting a person or couple who are respected in the community as honorary chairs opens the door to prospective donors, most notably among the chairs' circle of influence. "This year, both chairs were retired school teachers. We had groups of former students purchase sponsorships to support their favorite teachers," says Steil.

- **Go first class.** "Don't be afraid to provide many ways for the community to participate with in-kind donations," says Steil. Remember, the more they are personally involved, the more likely they are to attend the event.

- **Pay attention to details and encourage guests to share their experiences.** Be aware, for instance, of major sponsors who prefer non-alcoholic wine, vegetarian plates or who have food allergies. Keep lines moving quickly and speeches at a minimum (for Denim 'N' Diamonds the goal for speeches is under 20 minutes). Positive word-of-mouth is an effective marketing tool. By giving your guests good things to say to their family and friends about all aspects of your event — even the little details — you could be setting yourself up to reap the rewards in dollars and attendance at next year's event.

Source: Kathy Steil, Program Coordinator, Cheyenne Regional Medical Center Foundation, Cheyenne, WY. Phone (307) 633-7503. E-mail: Kathy.Steil@crmcwy.org

Toss the Bells and Whistles; Sponsors Want the Basics

In today's economy, securing sponsors for a special event can be a daunting task. Keeping those sponsors year after year can be even tougher.

Tony Poderis, fundraising consultant, recommends these tips to keep existing sponsors engaged:

- Acknowledge them promptly and in person if possible. Acknowledgement should include a letter signed by the board president or event chair, not a staff person.

- Show them results with a portfolio of all promotion and publicity for the event, with their name and logo prominently displayed.

- Inform them of the net profit, but only if it was a significant amount. If not, refer more generally to the net profit. This allows sponsors to learn about the real good your organization will be able to do, thanks to them.

- Let sponsors know the event couldn't have been a success without them.

Informing new sponsors of the business networking opportunities available to them also helps to secure their commitment. "It is a chance for them to meet and get the ears of another company's most important people," says Poderis. "Suddenly, they are sitting at a table with another company's CEO and spouse and that is a true networking opportunity."

Source: Tony Poderis, Fundraising Consultant, Willoughby Hills, OH. E-mail: tony@raise-funds.com

KEY STRATEGIES TO REALIZE MAJOR GIFTS

A major gift is defined differently by nonprofits depending on the organization's age, historical giving and the financial capability of its constituents. For many charities, a gift of $10,000 or $25,000 or more is considered a major gift. Of all fundraising efforts, major gifts hold the greatest potential. This chapter sets forth a system of prospect identification, research, cultivation, solicitation and stewardship you can follow to begin securing more major gifts.

Offer Language That Calls for Major Gifts

As you prepare to solicit persons capable of making six- and seven-figure gifts, it's worth contemplating the choice of messages and phrases you plan to convey during those all-important meetings.

Some examples of appropriate language may include:

- There is frankly no one more capable than you who can make this vision a reality.
- The ultimate success of this campaign will require an unprecedented gift.
- Your level of investment will set the pace for those gifts that follow.
- You are among that select handful of individuals who possess the ability to...
- Never in the history of our institution have we attempted to achieve such an extraordinary goal.

Prioritize Foundation Proposals

How do you determine which foundation proposals get written and submitted first? Here are three criteria that make sense for prioritizing proposal order:

1. **Program justification.** How important is the realization of the project in light of your mission and programs?
2. **Budgetary impact.** Will the resulting grant provide budget relief? Will it impose greater budget obligations?
3. **Fundraising potential.** How compelling would a foundation find the project to be?

Solicitation Calls: What Follows After Hearing Yes?

Your donor says yes to a major gift? Great! But be sure to take the proper steps to confirm the pledge before leaving the donor's office.

Jeff Miller, president and CEO, Junior Achievement of Central Indiana, Inc. (Indianapolis, IN), keeps a pledge form with him and uses it to capture the details of the gift before he leaves. He also makes sure the donor signs the form before he leaves.

The pledge form (shown in abbreviated format, below) includes what kind of recognition the donor will receive and a basic schedule of payments and dates.

"I'm quite detailed at this time because it is a lot tougher to go back if things are not very clear," says Miller. "I've learned that the word 'raised' on a matching pledge can mean something very different to the donor than it does to the recipient. To me, 'raised' means a signed pledge agreement. In Indiana, a signed pledge agreement is a legally enforceable instrument. However, a misunderstanding of one word can make a huge difference."

Once he returns to the office and types up the form, Miller makes a point to send, or if possible, hand-deliver, a copy as another opportunity to get face to face with the donor to further build the relationship.

Diana Humphrey, senior director of development, major gifts, Indiana University Kelley School of Business (Bloomington, IN), says that as soon as a donor says "yes," she gets the gift agreement or pledge form signed by the donor, school and foundation officials.

"I also talk to the donor about what their expectations are and what we have to offer them with regard to stewardship of their gift," she says.

The pledge form also includes information about matching funds; when the donor would like courtesy reminders and whether officials may announce the gift.

Source: Jeff Miller, President & CEO, Junior Achievement of Central Indiana, Inc., Indianapolis, IN. Phone (317) 252-5900, ext. 202. E-mail: jeff@jaindy.org
Diana Humphrey, Senior Director of Major Gifts, Indiana University, Bloomington, Kelley School of Business, Bloomington, IN. Phone (812) 855-6997.
E-mail: humphre@indiana.edu

The president and CEO of Junior Achievement of Central Indiana, Inc. (Indianapolis, IN) keeps this form on hand to capture specifics when a prospect says yes to a major gift:

Content not available in this edition

KEY STRATEGIES TO REALIZE MAJOR GIFTS

Develop a Plan of Cultivation for Each Prospect

Once you've identified those persons who are capable of making a major gift to your organization, it's wise to develop a plan for cultivating those individuals, businesses and/or foundations toward the realization of major gifts.

As you develop cultivation strategies for each prospect, keep in mind that each cultivation move: 1) should bring the prospect a step closer to saying "yes" 2) should be measured, 3) needs to includes some type of follow-up.

Moves can be as simple as sending a personal note or as complex as a week-long visit to the prospect's home. The potential size of a major gift, the personality of the prospect involved, and his/her interest in your organization all influence the degree and type of cultivation required.

Developing a cultivation plan for each prospect will help in moving that person closer to the realization of a major gift and will also help to better manage the cultivation of several major gift prospects over a period of time.

Make use of an individual cultivation plan such as the example shown at right to manage the cultivation process of multiple prospects.

INDIVIDUAL CULTIVATION PLAN
St. Joseph's Healthcare Foundation

Name _____ Date _____

Address _____ Phone _____

Prospect Manager _____

Staff/Volunteer(s) Assigned _____

Anticipated Solicitor(s) _____

Target Solicitation Date ____ Target Amount ____

Possible Use of Gift

1. _____ 4. _____
2. _____ 5. _____
3. _____ 6. _____

DATE	ANTICIPATED MOVE	BY WHOM	OUTCOME

Help Prospects Visualize Their Gifts' Impact

Selling something that won't exist until it's paid for can be challenging — a new building or a new program, for instance. How can you convince someone to put up $100,000 or more for something that he/she can't see, touch or fully experience?

Here's one way to do so: Use the past to sell the future. Help your prospects distinguish between now and then, before and after.

Whether you're selling a new building or a new program, point out what is being accomplished and not accomplished in the absence of the funding project. Then articulate — in terms they can understand — the impact the project will have once it is up and running. How will the completion of the project impact peoples' lives? How will it further your organization's reputation and enhance the community or region? What will the facility or program provide that currently is missing?

Selling dreams requires appealing to both the mind and the heart with heavier emphasis on the heart. Architectural drawings, facts, figures and charts help satisfy the intellectual needs of the prospect. Stories of how lives will be positively impacted, the good a new building or program will accomplish, appeal to the prospect's emotions.

Finally, sell smaller dreams first. If you're building a new science center, for instance, point out the real life benefits of a particular lab rather than dwelling on the benefits of the entire facility. Spoon-feeding smaller components of the overall project helps the prospect to better visualize and understand its multiple benefits.

Hesitant to Suggest A Gift Amount?

When setting the stage for a major gift, if you're hesitant about asking for a specific amount, use a chart that identifies levels of major gifts.

Referring to the chart, tell the prospect: "Picture yourself among this group of donors." By giving a level rather than an amount, you're setting out to negotiate a major gift commitment.

Offer Compelling Argument for Major Gifts Support

Need more ammunition for inviting major gift support? Add this powerful argument to your major gift solicitation repertoire:

"With the financial burdens currently facing the nation, you can be sure government funding for nonprofits will diminish. That's why support from the private sector is now more important than ever. Gifts from individuals, businesses and foundations were important during a thriving economy, but now it's critical if we are to maintain vital services."

KEY STRATEGIES TO REALIZE MAJOR GIFTS

Common Errors in Soliciting Major Gifts

There are many pitfalls that organizations can encounter when attempting to raise major gifts. Here are three common mistakes:

Error: Not asking for a specific amount. It is often difficult for an inexperienced volunteer to comfortably articulate an ask for a very significant sum.
Solution: Props can be helpful. A scale of gifts chart that indicates how many gifts are required at each level allows the solicitor to simply point to the appropriate level and ask for support in this range.

— Lisa Barnwell Williams,
Managing Partner,
Skystone Ryan Inc. (Cincinnati, OH)

Error: Not listening.
Solution: Instead of doing all the talking, ask questions that provide a chance for the potential donor to speak…and to speak from the heart. If you have done most of the talking in a solicitation, you have probably not listened to what the donor is really saying.

— Del Martin, Managing Partner
and Chairman,
Alexander Haas Martin and Partners
(Atlanta, GA)

Error: Failure to give the ask the deference it is due.
Solution: A request for a major gift — and the prospect from whom it is being requested — should be treated with the utmost respect. This means the request should be preceded with sufficient opportunity to interest and cultivate the prospective donor and that the ask is made in person in a setting where the prospect and solicitor clearly understand the purpose of the meeting.

— Jennifer Furla,
Executive Vice President,
Jeffrey Byrne and Associates, Inc.
(Kansas City, MO)

Know Where to Look for Prospects

Leave no stone unturned in your quest to identify individuals of means. Even though you may think every avenue has been exhausted, chances are you've missed something. Consider these obvious and not-so-obvious places to look:

- Past donors who have given at a certain dollar amount each year.
- Those who give repeatedly to your organization.
- Those who live in expensive homes or in wealthy neighborhoods. (Try sorting by ZIP code.)
- Those who maintain more than one home.
- Corporate officers/board members.
- Individuals and families whose names appear on statues, plaques, buildings or parks.
- Large landholders. See county plat books and property exchange records.
- Individuals with no apparent heirs.
- Philanthropists to other causes. Review other nonprofit organizations' lists of contributors.
- Social leaders — those active on boards or in community affairs.
- Those whose names appear on programs of cultural organizations.
- Obituary column of newspapers to determine spouses or children of wealthy persons.
- Prominent professionals. Check for mention in newspapers, newsletters and professional journals.
- Those active in their churches or synagogues.
- Referrals from board members, volunteers, staff, clients, donors and friends.
- Referrals from your vendors.
- Referrals from agents of wealth — attorneys, trust officers, accountants, insurance agents.

Make Your Organization Appealing to Major Gift Prospects

You really can't hope to attract major gifts unless programs and strategies are in place to invite such support. Improve your odds of attracting significant gifts by:

1. Getting major gift donors on your board.

2. Building exclusivity into your fundraising events.

3. Designing a donor upgrading system (e.g., gift clubs with corresponding benefits).

4. Involving prominent people on advisory committees.

5. Establishing a major gifts rating committee.

6. Having and using a public relations plan.

7. Making your budget understandable to prospects.

8. Developing a donor cultivation system.

9. Conducting an internal management audit.

10. Involving your community, and particularly major gift prospects, in planning.

11. Featuring prominent individuals in your literature (e.g., newsletters, brochures).

12. Preparing an attractive and compelling case statement.

13. Making your stationery, brochures and other printed materials look professional without appearing too extravagant or too cheap — give the impression that your organization is a class act, worthy of big gifts.

KEY STRATEGIES TO REALIZE MAJOR GIFTS

Grant Seeking for Rookies

Do you ever find yourself thinking about all the money that corporations and foundations give away each year and wonder how your organization can tap into those sources?

Have you tried to get funding through grant proposals but keep turning up empty handed? Or do you keep missing deadlines and lose those opportunities available to you?

Getting foundation funding requires extra effort, but the results can take your organization to the next level. The following guidelines and tips should help you get focused on this part of the fundraising picture.

Research — The first step in getting grants is to identify those foundations that will fund your type of organization and project. A number of resources are available with information on private, community and corporate foundations, and these often include details on past grant recipients and programs.

Look for funders whose priorities closely match your project, focusing on subject (arts, education, healthcare), type of support (scholarships, building campaigns, operating funds), and geographic areas (national, regional, statewide). You want to find foundations that intersect all of the areas that your organization's project does.

Also, look at past recipients and grant amounts for an idea of whether they have a history of funding organizations and projects like yours for the amounts you need.

You can manually search through directories or use electronic or CD-ROM resources to create lists of potential prospects. Check out area libraries and Foundation Center Collections if you don't have the resources in-house.

Request — Once you identify your prospects, it's always a good idea to get a copy of the foundations' guidelines, application forms and annual reports. Their funding priorities may have changed since the directories were published, and this is a way to make

sure your project fits before you write your proposal. You can call, write or, in many cases, get the information from their Web pages.

Write — Although each foundation has specific guidelines and requirements, you should have a base established for all your proposals. A proposal's main parts should consist of:

- An executive summary
- A statement of need for the project
- A description and time line of the project
- A budget outline, and
- General organization information.

Be concise and persuasive in your writing, and include only what information the foundation has requested.

Relationships — As with other types of fundraising, connections, ties and who you know can make a big difference in your success. If you have a board member or other supporter with connections to the foundation, have that individual personally send a follow-up letter in support of your proposal.

Contact the foundation during the proposal writing process. Program officers will often let you know ways to make your proposal more successful. They will also tell you if your project is most likely to not get funded by them. Both situations can save you a great deal of time. Try to visit them in person.

Once you get an answer from the foundation — positive or negative — follow up. If you are not funded, ask the program officer how you could change your proposal and when you can resubmit to the foundation. If you are funded, thank the foundation officials in writing and follow through with any project reporting requirements they have established.

Recognition — In addition to a standard gift acknowledgment, promote the gift among the community and your constituency. Work with the foundation to determine the level of publicity with which foundation officials are

comfortable. Marketing your success can often leverage additional funding from others. Good stewardship also leads to opportunities for future asks from the same foundation.

Record Keeping — The key to continued success is creating a system to identify appropriate prospects, keep the process working smoothly, ensure deadlines are not missed and help you develop relationships with your funders.

You should be able to track your prospects, including their interests, deadlines and contact information. Also include the results of your solicitations.

Record the dates, amounts and projects when you submit proposals.

Set up ticklers to remind you when decisions are due, when you should follow up with the foundations and as reminders of reporting requirement dates.

Regardless of whether your system is on index cards, a word processor or database software, it should not be overly complicated and should it fit your needs.

Judging Wealth, Gift Capability

Keep in mind the following information does not represent indisputable fact, but rather guidelines used to estimate an individual's ability to give:

1. A potential major gift might be calculated by multiplying the rate of an individual's consistent giving by 20 percent.
2. An appropriate major gift may be equal to 5 percent of a donor's known assets.
3. One way to estimate an individual's net worth is by multiplying his/her current salary by 10.
4. One estimate of giving ability is equal to 10 percent of stock and option holdings worth $1 million or more.

Fundraising for Beginners: Essential Procedures for Getting a Fundraising Program Up and Running

PLANNED GIVING 101

Planned gifts are those that are realized after a person's lifetime: bequests (the most popular form), charitable gift annuities, life insurance, charitable remainder trusts and more. This chapter will provide you with the framework to get a planned gifts program up and running, covering topics such as: 1) ways to promote planned gifts, 2) ideas for identifying and cultivating planned gift prospects, 3) ways to recognize planned gift donors and more.

Planned Giving in a One-person Shop

To be most effective in planned giving, a development officer should ideally commit at least a third of his or her time to this specialized area, says Marc Carmichael, president of R&R Newkirk Company, a planned giving consulting firm (Willow Springs, IL).

So what about the one-person shop in which the development officer wears many hats and may not have such time to devote to planned giving on an ongoing basis? Carmichael shares ways to maximize planned giving efforts in a small development office:

- **Become a one-person bequest solicitation program.** Get a basic wills brochure with a bequest phrase for your agency, or start a wills mailing program if you have the budget. Include bequest messages with every mailing (e.g., annual reports, thank-you letters, etc.). Start a wills society, with you and your board as charter members. At every opportunity, promote that you're in the business of accepting bequests. Change your stationary to include the tag line: "Have you included _____ in your will or living trust?" Send a survey card asking constituents if they 1) have include you in their wills or 2) will consider making a gift to you through their estate plans.

- **Include planned giving articles in your current publications.** Not a writer? Purchase copy only from publishers or find a volunteer to write for you.

- **Learn as much as you can about planned gift techniques.**

Attend a comprehensive planned gift training seminar, then attend at least one program a year that includes planned giving topics. Subscribe to a planned giving newsletter for fundraisers.

- **Touch base with your local community foundation,** where excellent help is often available, especially if you place endowed funds with the foundation.

- **Consider planned gift mailings,** but only if you can follow up. Consultants can allow you to extend your follow-up capabilities and provide technical expertise.

- **Conduct internal marketing with staff and your board** so they can provide planned gift referrals and make gifts themselves.

Source: Marc Carmichael, President, R&R Newkirk Company, Willow Springs, IL. Phone (800) 342-2375, ext. 302. E-mail: marccarmichael@msn.com

Rule of Thumb

- Expectancies are planned gift commitments known to have been made to your charity but not yet realized (because the donor is still living).

  As a guide only, you may assume that your charity is aware of one in six such expectancies in advance of receiving them. Example: If you know of 10 expectancies, there are probably at least 60 expectancies to be received at some point.

Conversation Tidbits

- Initiate a discussion by asking: "For what would you like to be remembered?"

- Close each conversation by asking: "Have you considered us with gifts in your will?"

Know Types of Charitable Bequests

Since bequests account for the single largest form of planned gift, it pays to become familiar with the broad types of charitable bequests that exist:

General bequest — Typically a charitable bequest with a specific dollar amount: "Pay [charity] $10,000 from my estate."

Specific bequest — A specific asset to be contributed from the deceased's estate: "Two hundred shares of Intel stock shall be given to [charity]."

Restricted bequest — Requires the bequest to be used for a specific project or program of interest to the donor.

Residuary bequest — Directs that all or a portion of the decedent's assets be directed to one or more charities after all debts, taxes, expenses and general and specific requests have been paid.

Percentage bequest — A stated percentage of the donor's estate or residuary estate is paid to one or more charities: "I give 30 percent of the rest and residue of my estate to [charity]."

Contingent bequest — Provides a gift to one or more charities in instances where the intended beneficiary either dies before the testator or the intended beneficiary disclaims a right to receive the testator's property at the time of death.

PLANNED GIVING 101

Basic Gift Planning: Start With These Giving Vehicles

The following gift planning vehicles should be a part of any planned giving program because they are the easiest for a new planned giving person to understand, says Pamela Davidson, president, Davidson Gift Design (Bloomington, IN):

Bequests. The easiest planned gift to make and accept. But remember, bequests have effect only at death and only if in a legally valid will or trust. A bequest in a valid will or trust can result in an estate tax deduction, which the individual may or may not need. As such, charities hope donors contact them about various lifetime charitable gift plans they can offer that can result in more income during life and an income tax deduction that donors could actually use, plus even provide income to a surviving spouse or partner among other planning advantages.

Revocable Beneficiary Designations, by a percentage, even modest, on one or more Qualified Retirement Plans. It is very expensive for children to inherit these, she says, so this asset should be the first considered for charitable giving. Qualified retirement plan assets are heavily taxed at some future time, with possible multiple income and estate and/or inheritance taxes, both state and federal, applied against the plan balance and before children inherit what's left. These combined taxes can, depending on other assets an individual owns, cost as much as 80 cents on the dollar or even more. These taxes can be avoided or reduced by using a charitable plan. An individual can designate a modest percentage to one or more charities simply by completing a beneficiary designation form provided by the company holding the plan, a revocable yet meaningful gift for individuals of all ages, says Davidson.

Gifts of Life Insurance. Some donors may no longer need a life insurance policy, which if owned by an individual at death, would be included in an estate for tax purposes, she says. If that policy

is no longer needed, an individual may give policy ownership during lifetime to a charity, which could qualify for an income tax deduction, or designate one or more charities for a percentage on a beneficiary designation form, a revocable choice.

Gifts of Appreciated Stock or Real Estate. If a donor uses part or all of a pre-tax asset like appreciated stock or real estate to fund a charitable plan, he or she can increase their tax and income advantages and make a larger philanthropic gift than they probably thought possible, she says. Using a pre-tax asset such as a certain number of stock shares or fractional percentage of real estate, directly to a charity or a charitable remainder trust, avoids capital gains taxes, meaning that the individual earns more income from the trust because more, without that tax payment, is invested. The donor also is entitled to an income tax deduction, and can even increase income since charitable remainder trusts must pay a return of at least five percent, and charitable gift annuities even more for older individuals.

Testamentary Disposition by Bequest of Government Savings Bonds, or Use During Life. Many individuals own U.S. savings bonds that no longer pay interest, which they don't cash in because of ordinary income recognition that can well result in income taxes, she says. Older individuals can cash these bonds in and make outright gifts to charity, with the charitable income tax deduction offsetting that ordinary income inclusion. They can even cash them in and fund a charitable life income arrangement like a trust or charitable gift annuity, with a partial income tax deduction that usually more than offsets the ordinary income inclusion while at the same time transforming a non-income producing asset into donor income.

Source: Pamela Jones Davidson, J.D., President, Davidson Gift Design, Bloomington, IN. Phone (812) 876-8646. E-mail: pjdavidson@giftplanners.com

Justify an Increase To Planned Gifts Budget

Whether you're attempting to establish a first-time planned gifts budget or hoping to enlarge it, here are three key criteria for justifying the needed funds:

1. What has been your organization's cost for previously received planned gifts? That cost-to-revenue ratio alone may make your case.

2. Compare your budget to the known amount of collective expectancies.

3. What's budgeted for donors making outright gifts of $10,000 or more?

Planned Gift Facts You Should Know

Did you know....

- Estates valued in excess of $1 million will likely include a charitable bequest?

- The likelihood of a charitable bequest is higher among surviving spouses than among the first to die?

- Eighty percent of individuals who contribute annually to charities do not have a will?

You Needn't be an Expert to Market Planned Gifts

- Did you know that about 80 percent of all planned gifts come in the form of bequests? That's why, no matter the size of your development shop, you don't need to be an expert to encourage and market planned gifts.

PLANNED GIVING 101

Create, Build on Your Planned Giving Program

Planned giving programs are vitally important to most nonprofit organizations, says Richard D. Barrett, president, Barrett Planned Giving, Inc. (Washington, DC).

After all, planned giving programs "are where the money is," Barrett says. However, "most organizations put off planned giving because it's not 'real money.' It's 'tomorrow money.' But if you wait a year to start, then it's one year plus tomorrow."

Barrett debunks several planned giving myths that he says can prevent nonprofits from moving forward. Here, he lays out those myths and explains why none of them should ever prevent an organization from getting on board with planned giving:

- **Myth: Planned giving is not appropriate for a new organization.** The donor's biggest question in this situation is, "You are brand new. How do I know you'll be there when the gift comes to fruition?" Adding a contingency to the donor's estate plan protects against this (e.g., "If this organization is no longer viable, the trustee or executor can give the gift to an organization of similar mission.")

- **Myth: Planned giving applies only to older people.** Younger people do estate planning, especially when faced with life transitions such as the birth of a child, death in the family or divorce.

- **Myth: I can't possibly think of planned giving when we need money *now!*** Planned gifts may be considered "tomorrow money," but they can help an organization get through dips in donations and secure its future.

- **Myth: I need more technical training/we need an experienced planned giving officer on staff/I**

Planned Giving Help Online

The following websites have resources and information to help you get started with or improve your planned giving program:

- www.barrettplannedgiving.com
- www.ncpg.org
- www.afpnet.org
- www.pgcalc.com

would be mortified if a donor asked a tax question I couldn't answer. These all speak to a skill set that need not necessarily be in place before moving forward, Barrett says. "Some of the most skilled lawyers answer questions with, 'I'll research that and get back to you.' There are resources and consultants that can help organizations and individuals answer the questions they don't know."

- **Myth: Planned giving hurts annual giving.** On the contrary, Barrett says that planned giving can increase annual giving. When a planned gift is made, the donor has a greater sense of ownership in the organization, cares more and gives more.

- **Myth: Our organization could never manage to pay a lifetime of checks.** You don't have to; banks and vendors will take on those tasks for you.

There's no good reason not to start a planned giving program, Barrett says. "Simply think about where you are now, where you want to go and how you will get there."

Source: Richard D. Barrett, President, Barrett Planned Giving, Inc., Washington, DC. Phone (202) 349-3812. E-mail: Richard@ BarrettPlannedGiving.com

Build a Capable Planned Gifts Committee

How many people do you have promoting planned gift opportunities or even identifying prospects on your behalf?

Regardless of your organization's size or level of fundraising sophistication, the development of a planned gifts committee can work wonders in expanding and achieving related objectives. Many valuable tasks are available for planned gift committees to take on and, in doing so, increase the number of planned gifts being realized by your organization. Here are just a few of those tasks:

1. Make personal planned gift provisions as examples to others.

2. Identify and refer the names of likely planned gift prospects from committee members' communities or circle of acquaintances.

3. Work to introduce planned gift prospects to your institution or agency and cultivate their interest.

4. Develop and approve policies related to planned gifts — types of gifts accepted, restrictions on planned gifts, investment policies, stewardship policies, etc.

5. Identify and establish rapport with agents of wealth — trust officers, attorneys, accountants, insurance agents and others.

6. Host receptions or banquets for those who have made planned gift provisions.

7. Identify appropriate ways of recognizing those who have made planned gifts.

PLANNED GIVING 101

An Idea for Planned Gift Expectancies

There are those persons who have indicated they've included your charity in their estate plans but have never made a significant outright gift. And there are those who have done both. To encourage the first group to consider making an outright gift (in addition to a planned gift), convince those who have done both to provide testimonials about why they are gratified they have made both outright and planned gifts to your cause.

Engage Your Board in Backing Planned Gifts Program

Your board's support (or lack of it) for your planned gifts program will impact its long-term success. Enthusiastic support can accelerate planned gifts tremendously.

Consider these steps to strengthen your board's commitment to and involvement in marketing planned gifts:

✓ Evaluate planned giving programs of nonprofits more advanced than yours and share finding with your board to raise your board's sights.

✓ Work with your board to establish planned gift goals. Engage members in shaping challenging yet realistic goals.

✓ Involve your board in establishing and evaluating a planned gifts policy. Does your nonprofit accept charitable remainder unitrusts? Should the board OK accepting bequests that include restrictions? Addressing such ongoing questions establishes the foundation of your planned gifts program and engages board members.

✓ Set a yearly calendar of activities and events inviting board participation: estate planning seminars, recognition of planned gift donors and more.

✓ Involve board members in shaping your planned giving budget. Share an itemized budget to show what you are able to accomplish plus additional resources could do.

✓ Recognize board members who give time and support to your planned gifts efforts to keep them motivated and also encourage others to become more involved.

✓ Meet one on one with board members to seek their input and expertise. Invite board members to make referrals and help in the cultivation of likely prospects.

✓ Invite individual board members to make planned gift commitments to your cause.

✓ Keep board members abreast of information affecting the world of planned giving: issues being addressed at the national level, demographics and more.

Establish Planned Gift Goals

Involve your board in establishing quantifiable objectives that move your program forward in securing new planned gifts. Consider goals such as:

❑ To identify ___ planned gift prospects in the current fiscal year.

❑ To average ___ personal visits each week with planned gift prospects.

❑ To solicit a minimum of ___ planned gifts throughout the current fiscal year.

❑ To secure ___ planned gift expectancies amounting to at least $___ during the current fiscal year.

❑ To expand the planned gifts mailing list by ___ during the current year.

❑ To conduct ___ estate planning seminars during the current year.

❑ To enlist ___ centers of influence who will assist our planned gifts efforts by identifying and cultivating would-be donors.

❑ To invite all board members to consider our charity in estate plans.

Use History, Demographics to Set Planned Gift Goals

Because of the wide fluctuations that inevitably occur in realized planned gifts from year to year, it can be especially challenging to set goals for what you might hope to achieve in the way of planned gifts. However, once a program has been up and running for five or more years, you should be able to set some quantifiable objectives based on a combination of past history and estimated projections:

1. Depending on how long your planned gift program has been in place, determine your organization's five- or 10-year average for realized planned gifts — in terms of both dollar amounts received and number of planned gifts.

2. Based on planned gift expectancies you are aware of, you can produce an in-house schedule of anticipated gifts based on donors' ages and life expectancy tables.

3. If you're able to determine the approximate ages of those in your database, you can get some sense of the number of 65-and-older constituents at present compared to future numbers of those in that same age group. This will allow you to anticipate the size of your prospect pool at any given time with age being the primary factor.

PLANNED GIVING 101

Help Planned Gift Prospects Visualize What They Are Capable of Doing

Most planned gifts are driven by some form of personal gratification — to help others and society, to leave a lasting legacy, to honor or memorialize someone.

A donor's ability to visualize what his/her gift will accomplish is key to making that gift a reality.

Your preparation in painting a picture of what a planned gift will accomplish for your institution and those you serve will help the prospect begin to experience the personal need — helping others, making a difference, ego gratification — that will make the individual want to make a bequest or some other form of a planned gift.

That's why it's so important to visualize what could be as you meet with and cultivate planned gift prospects. It's not enough to know the technical aspects and tax consequences of various planned gifts. You need to also take steps to help the prospect actually see how his/her planned gift could make a noticeable difference:

- Provide personal tours of your facilities, pointing out present services and comparing them to what could be offered with the realization of a major gift.

- As you meet with prospects, share printed illustrations of named gift opportunities that you can leave with them. One illustration may, for instance, describe what a $50,000 gift could accomplish in providing annual scholarships for needy students. Another may help to visualize how an endowed landscaping and maintenance fund will enhance your organization's environment and maintain it for years to come.

- Share specific examples of what past donors' bequests are accomplishing for your organization. In fact, share examples of what other donors' planned gifts have accomplished for other institutions. This is simply another way of visualizing what could happen if sufficient funds were made available.

In addition to helping donors see just what their gifts will accomplish, it's important to help them visualize the mechanics of how their gift is spent or invested (as in the case of an endowed gift). The more they understand, the more comfortable they will become in turning visions into reality.

Sample personalized illustration of a naming gift opportunity.

Connect With Persons Of Means

One fact always remains true: you can only get money from people who have it to give. The more people you have associated with your organization who have financial resources, the better your chances will be of successfully soliciting and closing major gifts. Building relationships with people of affluence and influence should be a top priority.

Cosgrove University
Preparing Tomorrow's Leaders Today

NAMING GIFT CONSIDERATION

THE MARGARET AND TAYLOR ELLINGSON ENDOWED SCHOLARSHIP

Suggested Gift Amount: $100,000

Intent of Bequest

To assist Junior and Senior women attending Cosgrove University who intend to pursue health-related careers. Eligible students must have maintained a 3.4 grade point average or higher during their Freshman and Sophomore years. Financial need should also be taken into consideration.

How the Funds Will Be Invested

Once this $100,000 bequest is realized, it will be invested as a part of Cosgrove University's endowment portfolio. (See attached endowment report.) Annual interest from the fund will be awarded to deserving students who meet the guidelines set forth by Margaret and Taylor Ellingson. In recent years, the university's board of directors has approved an annual payout of 7 percent to ensure the preservation of the gift's principal for generations to come.

Therefore, if the annual interest rate remains constant, $7,000 will be available each year for scholarship awards.

Procedure for Annual Awards

At the request of Margaret and Taylor Ellingson, annual awards will be made through the Office of Financial Aid in cooperation with faculty representatives from the science/health-related disciplines.

Preparing Future Generations of Caring Health Professionals

Consider, for example, seven deserving Cosgrove University students each receiving a $1,000 award in any given year. Using that example, a gift such as this could potentially assist as many as 70 students throughout one decade receive a degree who might not otherwise be able to do so.

Over a 10-year period, as many as 70 graduates could be moving on to seek additional education or entering health-related careers. What a marvelous way to help so many young people! What a marvelous investment in our society's future!

PLANNED GIVING 101

Get Your Feet Wet With Planned Giving

So you're ready to delve into planned giving, but you aren't sure where to start?

Richard D. Barrett, president, Barrett Planned Giving, Inc. (Washington, DC), offers the following tips to make sure you're headed in the right direction:

- **Start simple.** Depending on your resources, taking on a full-fledged planned giving program could be challenging. But getting started can be as simple as putting a footer on your stationary. Something like, "Please consider this organization in your estate plans," can lead to bequests. Barrett says most planned giving money comes in the form of bequests and, because they are easy to manage, are a great place to begin.

- **Guard your mailing lists with your life.** Make sure you know the financial professionals you are working with and that they know your expectations. Make

it clear the information they may glean when doing an informational session for your donors or prospective donors is off limits for their professional gain.

- **Set up a Legacy Society.** Barrett says Legacy Societies (or whatever name you choose) help to recognize those who have made planned gifts to your organization. Persons who are part of a society are less likely to take your organization out of their estate plans.

- **Do not become a trustee of trusts.** Trusts should be handled by a trustee of the donor's choice — for instance, a bank trust department — he says. "There is significant conflict of interest when the recipient is also the trustee."

Source: Richard D. Barrett, President, Barrett Planned Giving, Inc., Washington, DC. Phone (202) 349-3812. E-mail: Richard@BarrettPlannedGiving.com

Starting From Scratch? Build a Planned Gifts Prospect List

If you're just getting started with a planned gifts program, a key first step is to build a database of qualified names.

While those persons on your mailing list who have reached retirement make obvious prospects, it's important to screen and rescreen your list. Likewise, age should not prevent someone from being added. After all, life insurance is one of the most affordable major gifts a young person can make.

As you review names to be added to your list, consider:

- ✓ Individuals or married couples with no apparent heirs. This characteristic, when combined with senior citizen status, represents obvious candidates for planned gifts.

- ✓ Current and former longtime employees.

- ✓ Persons who have served as volunteers or board members or received awards from your organization in past years.

- ✓ Those who have made consistent gifts to your organization over a long period of time, regardless of size.

- ✓ Those who support many nonprofits in your community, as this proven level of philanthropy may qualify them as planned gift prospects.

- ✓ Agents of wealth: trust officers, attorneys, accountants, insurance agents and other financial planners. While these professionals may not make a planned gift themselves, they can be helpful in influencing others by virtue of association with your organization.

Don't Hesitate To Get Expert Advice

If you're not an expert at planned gifts, don't attempt to answer prospects' questions if you're unsure of the answers. Instead, take the time to get the right answers. After all, planned gifts should be the result of careful consideration on the part of the donor, and your goal should be to help the donor arrive at a decision that he/she will feel positive about months and even years later.

Should a technical question arise, respond genuinely: "That's a good question, but one I need to research in order to give you the best possible advice. Let me get back to you on that one."

Then do whatever it takes to provide a knowledgable response: Research, meet with an attorney or planned gift expert or get the right professional involved with the prospect. Your primary goal, even beyond securing a planned gift, should be to assist the prospect to arrive at the best possible decision for him/her.

How to Ask for an Unspecified Bequest

You've just learned that a planned gift prospect has included your charity in her estate plans. How can you learn the size of her gift without appearing nosey?

Here's one approach:

Ask the donor if she has given thought as to how the bequest should be used when your organization receives it. Using this approach, you can then go into various levels of gifts required for various projects based on the donor's response.

This gentle probing style may result in discovering the bequest amount.

Lightning Source UK Ltd.
Milton Keynes UK
UKOW02f0609200813

215640UK00006B/147/P